D0479437

INSTANT GUIDE

San Francisco
Berkeley • Oakland • Bay Area

3-89   88
SALE
$ 1 99

The idea of SINGLE SUBJECT MAPS with related material was conceived by FLASHMAPS Publications in 1967. A single-subject map, color-coded and cross-indexed, has proven to be a useful tool for clearly dispensing information. FLASHMAPS INSTANT GUIDE books are used by both natives and visitors alike to save time, money and energy.

ENJOY SAN FRANCISCO!

PUBLISHED and DISTRIBUTED by

FLASHMAPS PUBLICATIONS, Inc.

PUBLISHER and EDITOR:
 Toy Lasker
CARTOGRAPHERS:
 Timothy W. Lasker
 Sally Jarman
DIRECTOR of RESEARCH:
 Gladys F. Caterinicchio

ISSN 0277-6065
ISBN 0-942226-05-4
Manufactured in the United States of America

TABLE OF CONTENTS

IMPORTANT TELEPHONE NUMBERS (Area Code 415)

EMERGENCIES

Ambulance	911	Gas & Elec Emerg	981-3232
Fire	911	Highway Patrol	O-Zenith 1-2000
Police	911	Medical Help	431-2800
Fire Headquarters	861-8000	Poison Control	666-2845
Police Headquarters	553-0123	Rape Help Line	647-7273
Child Abuse	665-0757	Sewer Emergency	558-3271
Drug Abuse	673-6799	Sherrif's Office	558-2411
CIA	986-0145	Suicide Prevention	221-1423
Coast Guard	556-2103	U S Secret Service	556-6800
FBI	552-2155	Water Emergency	558-4101

SERVICES
(Civic Center Government Offices, Telephones Page 75)

Adoption	557-5376	Mayor's Office	558-3456
Air Polution	771-6000	Mental Health	387-5100
Alcoholics Anonymous	661-1828	Muir Woods Natl Mon	388-2595
Animal Bites	558-4046	MUNI	673-6864
Art Commission	558-3463	National Park Service	556-4122
BART	788-2278	Parking Authority	558-3651
Battered Women Help	864-4722	Parks & Recreation	558-3706
Better Business Bureau	775-3300	Passport Info	974-7972
Birth Control	441-7767	Performing Arts Ctr	621-6600
Board of Education	565-9000	Planned Parenthood	441-5454
Central Library	558-3191	Port of SF	391-8000
Chamber of Commerce	392-4511	Post Office	556-2051
City Jail	553-1441	Presidio of SF	561-2211
Cliff House Visitors Ctr	386-3330	Public Health	558-3131
Consumer Affairs	777-9635	Public Schools	565-9000
Customs Info	556-4440	Public Works Action Line	558-2142
Drug Enforcement	556-6771	Senior Citizens	558-4952
Drug Help Info	752-3400	SF Information	558-6161
Equal Opportunity	556-0260	SF Municipal Court	558-4041
Federal Information	556-6600	SF Visitors Conv Bur	974-6900
Fed Govt Bookstore	556-6657	Sherrif's Dept	558-2411
Food & Drug	556-2062	Ship Info	765-6661
Food Stamps Info	557-5000	Social Security Medicare	956-3000
Fort Point Historic Site	556-2857	Taxes: Federal	839-1040
Golden Gate Natl Rec	556-0560	City/County	558-3507
Golden Gate Park	558-3706	Telegrams/Cables	433-5520
Harbor Master	563-8300	Traffic Fines	553-1662
Highway Dept	557-1094	Traveler's Aid	781-6738
Housing Authority	673-5800	Veterans Administration	495-8900
Immigration Information	556-2070	Voter Registration Info	558-3417
Marriage License	558-3969	Youth Guidance Center	731-5740

RECORDED MESSAGES

Academy of Sciences	752-8268	Sports Scoreboard	(900) 555-1212
Daily Events	391-2000	Time	767-8900
Dial-A-Meditation	665-2244	Weather	936-1212
Dial-A-Prayer	664-7729	Zoological Gardens	661-4844

SAN FRANCISCO WEATHER

	Average High	Average Low	Average Temperature	Total No. Rain Days
WINTER Dec thru Feb	57.1	46.3	51.5	10.66
SPRING March thru May	62.4	49.3	55.5	6.66
SUMMER June thru August	65.3	52.6	59.5	.66
FALL Sept thru Nov	66.6	53.3	60.5	4.33

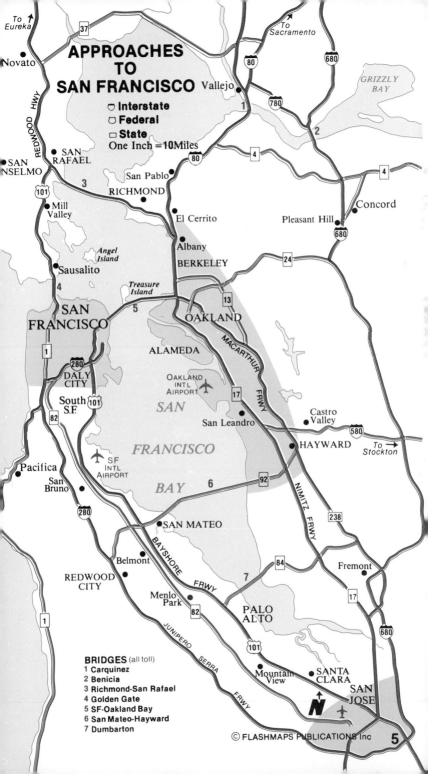

APPROACHES TO SAN FRANCISCO

◯ **Interstate**
◯ **Federal**
▢ **State**
One Inch = 10 Miles

To Eureka
Novato
To Sacramento
Vallejo
GRIZZLY BAY
San Rafael
SAN NSELMO
San Pablo
RICHMOND
Concord
Pleasant Hill
Mill Valley
El Cerrito
Angel Island
Albany
BERKELEY
Sausalito
Treasure Island
SAN FRANCISCO
OAKLAND
ALAMEDA
MACARTHUR FRWY
DALY CITY
Oakland Intl Airport
South S.F.
SAN FRANCISCO BAY
San Leandro
Castro Valley
HAYWARD
To Stockton
Pacifica
San Bruno
SF Intl Airport
NIMITZ FRWY
San Mateo
Belmont
REDWOOD CITY
Fremont
BAYSHORE FRWY
Menlo Park
PALO ALTO
JUNIPERO SERRA FRWY
Mountain View
SANTA CLARA
SAN JOSE

BRIDGES (all toll)
1 Carquinez
2 Benicia
3 Richmond-San Rafael
4 Golden Gate
5 SF-Oakland Bay
6 San Mateo-Hayward
7 Dumbarton

© FLASHMAPS PUBLICATIONS Inc

5

SAN FRANCISCO INTERNATIONAL AIRPORT

NORTH TERMINAL

E

BUTLER AVIATION

F

INTERNATL TERMINAL

LONG TERM PARKING

To San Francisco

US 101

PARKING

D

BUDGET | DOLLAR

GARAGE

HERTZ | AVIS

NATIONAL

C

SOUTH TERMINAL

AIRPORT HILTON

US 101

To San Jose

ROTUNDA

A

B

N

© FLASHMAPS PUBLICATIONS Inc.

AIRLINES

Airline	Area	Telephone	Airline	Area	Telephone
Air Cal	E	433-2660	Northwest	D	392-2163
Air Canada	F	(800) 422-6232	PSA	E	956-8636
Alaska	B	(800) 426-0333	Pacific Coast	E	(800) 322-8811
American	E	398-4434	Pan American	D	397-5200
Braniff	F	877-0400	Philippine Air	D	391-0470
British	D	362-5595	Piedmont	E	978-9663
CAAC	D	392-2156	Qantas	D	761-8000
China	D	989-3300	Republic	B	362-1110
Continental	B	989-3370	SFO Helicopter	F	430-8666
CP Air	D	391-0880	Singapore	D	(800) 642-3333
Delta	E	552-5700	Southwest	B	885-1221
Eastern	F	474-5858	TACA	D	398-5231
Frontier	E	(800) 255-5050	TWA	B	864-5731
Hawaii Air	B	(800) 697-4085	US Air	B	(800) 428-4322
Horizon	B	(800) 547-9308	United	F	397-2100
Japan Air	D	982-8141	Westair	F	(800) 338-1111
LTU	D	873-1907	Western	B	(800) 227-6105
Lufthansa	D	(800) 645-3880	Wings West	B	(800)-252-0017
Mexicana	D	(800) 531-7921			

TRANSPORTATION TO/FROM AIRPORT

Airporter Coach Line: To downtown SF terminal- Taylor & Ellis (673-2432)
5:20 AM-9:20 PM EVERY 10/20 MINS   9:20 PM-5:20 AM EVERY 35/45 MINS   FARE: $6.00
Shuttle Bus: All terminals, economy parking and car rental
Taxis: To/From downtown San Francisco
YELLOW (861-7291) DE SOTO (673-1414) LUXOR (552-4040) VETERANS (552-1300) FARE: $20-$35
SamTrans: Local stops to downtown SF (761-7000) - Fare: $1.15
SFO/Oak Bus: Bay Area Service Co (632-5506) - Fare: $7.00

SAN FRANCISCO AREA AIRPORTS

Marin County-Gnoss Field	Novato, California	897-1754
Oakland International	Hegenberger Rd, Oakland	577-4000
San Jose Municipal	1551 Airport Blvd San Jose	(408) 277-4000

6

PIERS & TERMINALS
CABLE CARS

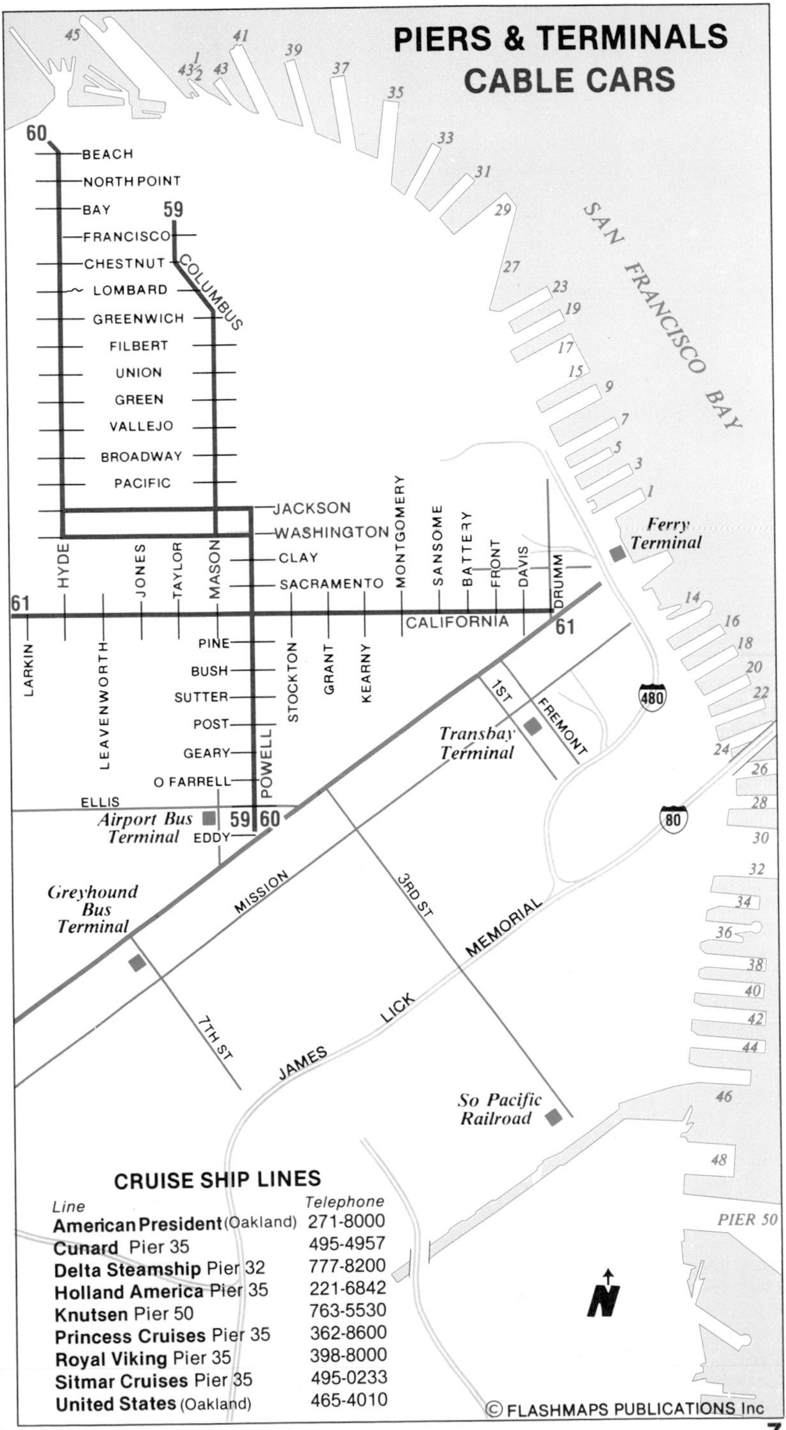
SAN FRANCISCO BAY
Ferry Terminal
Transbay Terminal
Airport Bus Terminal
Greyhound Bus Terminal
So Pacific Railroad
PIER 50
BEACH
NORTH POINT
BAY
FRANCISCO
CHESTNUT
LOMBARD
GREENWICH
FILBERT
UNION
GREEN
VALLEJO
BROADWAY
PACIFIC
JACKSON
WASHINGTON
CLAY
SACRAMENTO
CALIFORNIA
PINE
BUSH
SUTTER
POST
GEARY
O FARRELL
ELLIS
EDDY
COLUMBUS
HYDE
JONES
TAYLOR
MASON
POWELL
LARKIN
LEAVENWORTH
STOCKTON
GRANT
KEARNY
MONTGOMERY
SANSOME
BATTERY
FRONT
DAVIS
DRUMM
1ST
FREMONT
MISSION
3RD ST
7TH ST
JAMES LICK MEMORIAL
480
80
59
60
61
N
© FLASHMAPS PUBLICATIONS Inc

CRUISE SHIP LINES

Line	*Telephone*
American President (Oakland)	271-8000
Cunard Pier 35	495-4957
Delta Steamship Pier 32	777-8200
Holland America Pier 35	221-6842
Knutsen Pier 50	763-5530
Princess Cruises Pier 35	362-8600
Royal Viking Pier 35	398-8000
Sitmar Cruises Pier 35	495-0233
United States (Oakland)	465-4010

DOWNTOWN STREETS

15

16

HYDE

19 JEFFERSON

20 BEACH

21 NORTH POINT

22 VAN NESS

23 BAY

24 FRANCISCO

25 CHESTNUT

26 LOMBARD

27 GREENWICH

28 FILBERT

29 UNION

30 GREEN

31 VALLEJO

32 BROADWAY

33 PACIFIC

34 JACKSON

35 WASHINGTON

36 CLAY

37 SACRAMENTO

38 CALIFORNIA

39 PINE

40 BUSH

41 SUTTER

42 POST

43 GEARY

44 O'FARRELL

45 ELLIS

46 EDDY

47 TURK

48 GOLDEN GATE

49 MCALLISTER

50 FULTON

51 GROVE

52 HAYES

53 FELL

54 OAK

55 PAGE

57

POLK

LARKIN

2800

800

1000

3000

2700

900

3000

1400

2700

1100

2200

2700

1300

1500

2700

2400

1100

2700

2400

1200

1900

2400

1300

2400

1500

2100

1200

1600

2100

1300

1800

2100

1500

1600

2100

1600

1800

1300

2100

1800

1500

1900

1800

1600

300

1800

1700

1500

1400

1700

1500

1400

1700

1500

1400

1000

1500

1400

1200

1100

1500

1300

1200

1000

1300

1200

1000

700

1200

1000

900

700

1000

900

700

1000

900

700

400

900

900

700

600

400

700

600

400

600

400

100

400

300

100

600

100

CIVIC CENTER

8TH

1100

400

200

100

58

MARKET

9TH ST

100

300

GOUGH

FRANKLIN

10TH ST

100

11TH ST

100

8

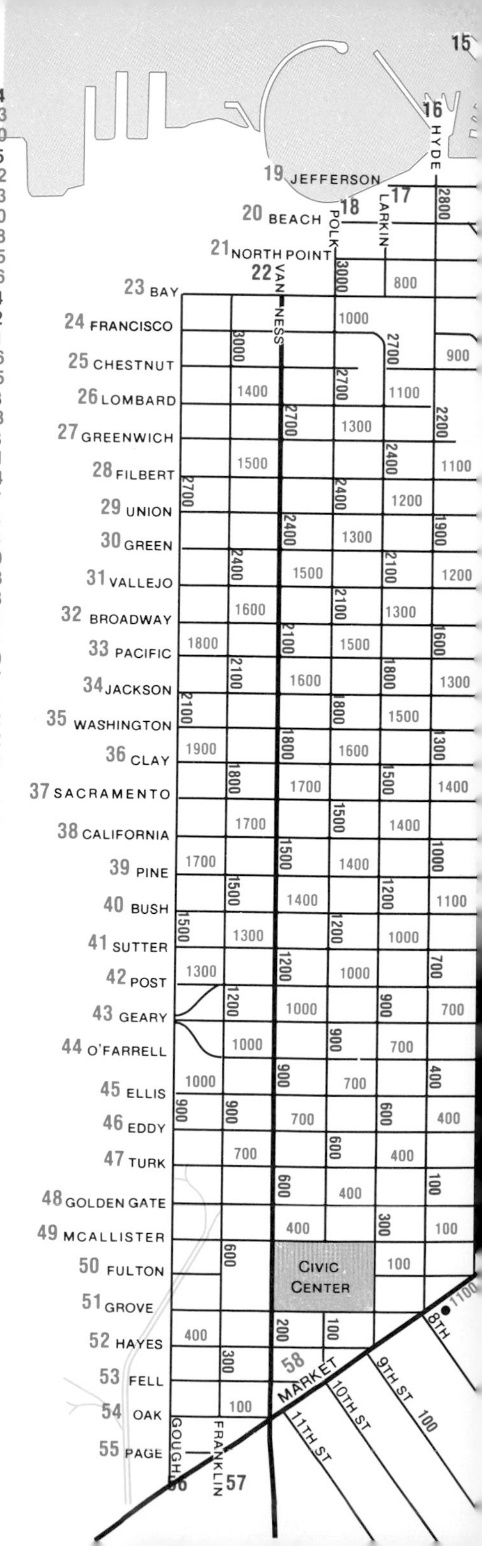

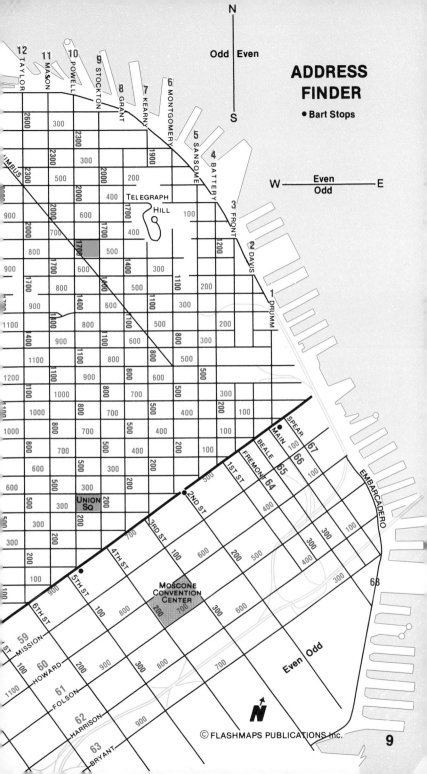

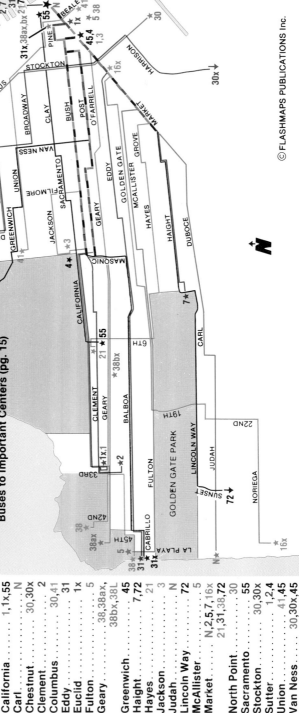

BUSES EAST/WEST
IN to
DOWNTOWN SF

X—Express Bus only
Bus Information: 673-MUNI
Buses to Important Centers (pg. 15)

© FLASHMAPS PUBLICATIONS Inc.

BUSES EAST & WEST
IN & OUT—Pg 10 & 11

Street	Bus No
Balboa	31,31x,38
Broadway	30x
California	1,1x,55
Carl	N
Chestnut	30,30x
Clement	2
Columbus	30,41
Eddy	31
Euclid	1x
Fulton	5
Geary	38,38ax, 38bx,38L
Greenwich	45
Haight	7,72
Hayes	21
Jackson	3
Judah	N
Lincoln Way	72
McAllister	5
Market	N,2,5,7,16x 21,31,38,72
North Point	30
Sacramento	55
Stockton	30,30x
Sutter	1,2,4
Union	41,45
Van Ness	30,30x,45

BUSES EAST/WEST
OUT of DOWNTOWN SF

X — Express Bus only
Bus Information: 673-MUNI
Buses to Important Centers (pg. 15)

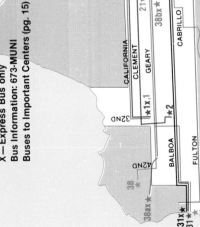

**BUSES EAST & WEST
IN only—Page 10**

Street	Bus No
Bush	1x,31x, 38ax,38bx
Clay	55
Divisadero	30,30x
Fourth	30,30x
Golden Gate	16x
Grove	21
Harrison	30x
O'Farrell	38,38L
Page	7,72
Post	1,2,3,4,45

OUT only—Page 11

Bryant	30x
Pine	1x,31x, 38ax,38bx
Third	30x,30
Townsend	30
Turk	16x

© FLASHMAPS PUBLICATIONS Inc.

11

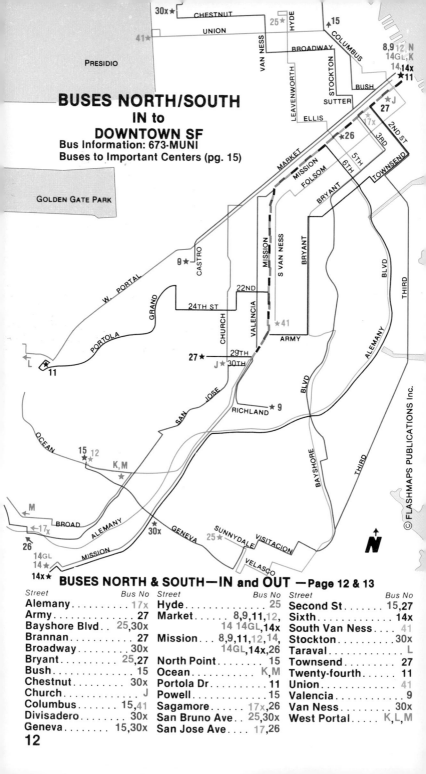

BUSES NORTH/SOUTH
IN to
DOWNTOWN SF
Bus Information: 673-MUNI
Buses to Important Centers (pg. 15)

GOLDEN GATE PARK

PRESIDIO

BUSES NORTH & SOUTH—IN and OUT —Page 12 & 13

Street	Bus No	Street	Bus No	Street	Bus No
Alemany	17x	Hyde	25	Second St	15,27
Army	27	Market	8,9,11,12,	Sixth	14x
Bayshore Blvd	25,30x		14 14GL,14x	South Van Ness	41
Brannan	27	Mission	8,9,11,12,14,	Stockton	30x
Broadway	30x		14GL,14x,26	Taraval	L
Bryant	25,27	North Point	15	Townsend	27
Bush	15	Ocean	K,M	Twenty-fourth	11
Chestnut	30x	Portola Dr	11	Union	41
Church	J	Powell	15	Valencia	9
Columbus	15,41	Sagamore	17x,26	Van Ness	30x
Divisadero	30x	San Bruno Ave	25,30x	West Portal	K,L,M
Geneva	15,30x	San Jose Ave	17,26		

© FLASHMAPS PUBLICATIONS Inc.

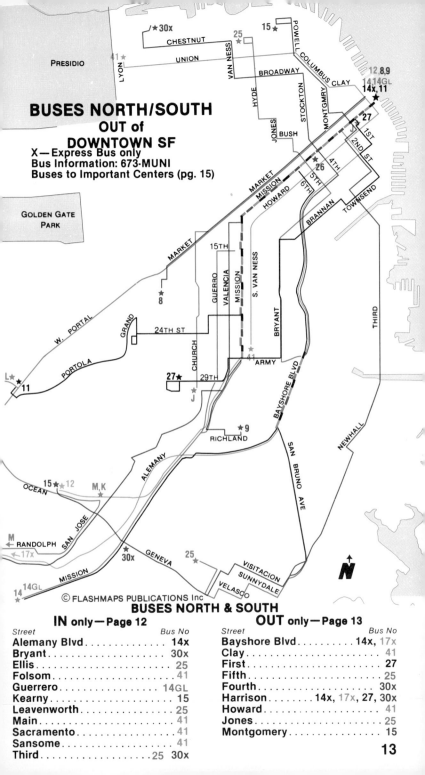

BUSES NORTH/SOUTH
OUT of
DOWNTOWN SF
X—Express Bus only
Bus Information: 673-MUNI
Buses to Important Centers (pg. 15)

© FLASHMAPS PUBLICATIONS Inc

BUSES NORTH & SOUTH

IN only—Page 12	
Street	*Bus No*
Alemany Blvd	**14x**
Bryant	**30x**
Ellis	**25**
Folsom	**41**
Guerrero	**14GL**
Kearny	**15**
Leavenworth	**25**
Main	**41**
Sacramento	**41**
Sansome	**41**
Third	**25 30x**

OUT only—Page 13	
Street	*Bus No*
Bayshore Blvd	**14x, 17x**
Clay	**41**
First	**27**
Fifth	**25**
Fourth	**30x**
Harrison	**14x, 17x, 27, 30x**
Howard	**41**
Jones	**25**
Montgomery	**15**

13

BUSES (Not Downtown)

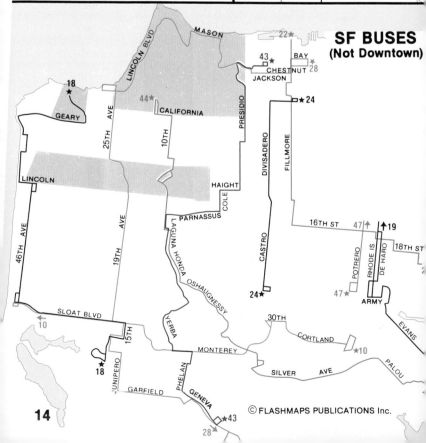

SF BUSES Circling DOWNTOWN

SF BUSES (Not Downtown)

14

© FLASHMAPS PUBLICATIONS Inc.

BART • BUSES • CABLE CARS TO IMPORTANT CENTERS

Center	Public transportation
Academy of Science	5,19,38 to 44
Aquatic Park	19,30,32
Arboretum	5,19,38
Asian Art	5,19,38 to 44
Balboa Pk Stad	K Balboa PK Sta
Cable Car Museum	cc60
CA Mines Geo	2,Ferry Embar Sta
CA Historical Soc	30,38 to 25
CA Soc Pioneers	5 Civ Center Sta
CA University	K to M
Candlestick Park	30
Cannery	30,32,cc60
Chinatown	30,61
Chinese Cultural	15
Civic Aud	5,21 Civ Ctr sta
Civic Center	5,21 Civ Ctr sta
Cliff House	2,38,38L,N
Coit Tower	30,39
Cow Palace	25
Curran Thea	30,38,59,cc60 Civ Ctr
Davies Hall	5,21 Civ Ctr sta
De Young Museum	5,19,38 to 44
Embarcadero Cntr	2,6,8,61 Embarc
Energy Expo	2
Exploratorium	30
Ferry Bldg	2,Embarcad
Fisherman's Wharf	19,32,59,cc60
Fort Mason	4,28,30,42
Fort Point	28, to GG
Ghiradelli Square	30,32,cc60
GG Bridge	30 to 28
GG Park	5,10,19,38,44,47,71,
Golden Gate Univ	9,11,12,26
Grace Cathedral	59, ,cc61
Haas Lilienthal	45
Hastings College	5,21, Civ Ctr Sta
Hyde St Pier	19,32,cc60
Jack London Sq	
Japan Center	1,2,3,4
Japan Tea Garden	38 to 44
Kezar Stadium	71,72
Lincoln Pk	2,31,47
Lincoln Univ	6,7,66
Lombard Street	30, cc60

Center	Public Transportation
Marina District	30,47
Maritime Mus	19,30,32,cc60
Mexican Mus	12,1 16th St Sta
Mission Dolores	J 16th St Sta
Morrison Planetarium	5,19,38 to 44
Nob Hill	59,cc60/61 Montgmry sta
North Beach	15,30
Oakland Mus	Lake Merritt sta
Oakland Coliseum	Coliseum sta
Oakland Airport	Airporter
Ocean Beach	2,5,38,38L,N
Octagon House	45
Old Mint	59,cc60 Powell St Sta
Orpheum Theater	5,21 Civ Ctr Sta
Palace Fine Arts	30
Palace Legion Honor	2
Perform Arts Ctr	5,21 Civ Ctr Sta
Pioneer Memorial Museum	2
Presidio Army Museum	45
Russian Hill	cc60
Seal Rocks	38,38L
SF Art Institute	30,30x
SF City College	K to L-M Balboa sta
SF Internatl Airport	Airporter
SF Mus Mod Art	5,21, Civ Ctr sta
SF Gen Hosp	47
Simpson College	13,44
St Mary's Cathedral	38
Steinhart Aquarium	5,19,38 to 44
Stern Music Grove	K
Telegraph Hill	15,30,39
Twin peaks	K to 36
U of CA Berkeley	F
U of CA Exten	1,2,3,31
U of CA Med Center	6,66
U of CA San Francisco	5
Union Street	45,47
Union Square	30,38,59,cc60
	Montgomery/Powell Sta
War Mem Opera House	5,21
	Civ Ctr sta
Wells Fargo Mus	45,Montgmry sta
Wine Museum	32,cc60
Zoo	K to L-M

TRANSPORTATION INFORMATION:

AC Transit	839-2882	GG Ferry	332-6600	SamTrans	761-7000
Airporter	673-2432	GG Transit	332-6600	San MateoTrans	761-7000
Alcatraz	546-2885	Greyhound	433-1500	So Pacific RR	492-4546
AMTRAK	982-8512	Larkspur Ferry	332-6600	SF Airport	761-0800
Angel Is Ferry	546-2815	MUNI	673-6864	Tiburon Ferry	546-2815
BART	788-2278	Oakland Airport	577-4000	Trailways	982-6400

15

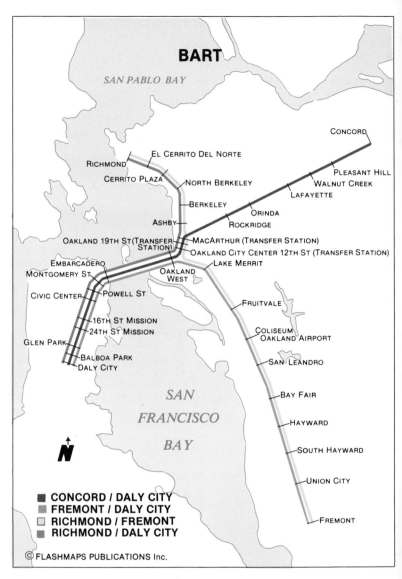

BART

SAN PABLO BAY

CONCORD

EL CERRITO DEL NORTE

RICHMOND

PLEASANT HILL

CERRITO PLAZA

NORTH BERKELEY

WALNUT CREEK

LAFAYETTE

BERKELEY

ORINDA

ASHBY

ROCKRIDGE

OAKLAND 19TH ST(TRANSFER STATION)

MACARTHUR (TRANSFER STATION)

OAKLAND CITY CENTER 12TH ST (TRANSFER STATION)

EMBARCADERO

LAKE MERRIT

MONTGOMERY ST

OAKLAND WEST

CIVIC CENTER

POWELL ST

FRUITVALE

16TH ST MISSION

24TH ST MISSION

COLISEUM

OAKLAND AIRPORT

GLEN PARK

BALBOA PARK

SAN LEANDRO

DALY CITY

SAN

FRANCISCO

BAY FAIR

BAY

HAYWARD

SOUTH HAYWARD

UNION CITY

■ **CONCORD / DALY CITY**
■ **FREMONT / DALY CITY**
□ **RICHMOND / FREMONT**
■ **RICHMOND / DALY CITY**

FREMONT

© FLASHMAPS PUBLICATIONS Inc.

BART FACTS AND INFORMATION

Time: Mon-Sat 6:00 am to 12:00 pm
Sunday- 9:00 am to 12:00 pm

Fare: $.60 to $2.15 (according to distance)

Ticket Information:

DISCOUNT - Senior Citizens, Handicapped
Children 5 to 12 yrs(4 & under free)

Telephone Information

SF . . . 464-7135   SSF 788-BART
TTY . . 839-2220   Oakland . 465-BART
BANKS - sell multi ride & discount tickets

PURCHASE: min $.60   max $20
Ticket Machine in all BART stations
(5, 10, 25 cent coins — $1.00 & $5.00 bills)

Ticket Use: Insert ticket to enter train.
Insert ticket to exit — Fare is deducted.
(if ticket is rejected go to AddFare machine
and pay amount due)

Pets: Only pets in carrying cases
and Guide and Signal dogs

Bikes: With permit - Sat & Sun all day
Mon thru Fri non-commute hours

BART STATIONS & LINES—ALPHABETICAL

Bart Station	Approximate Location	Line (Color coded for clarity)
Ashby	Adeline and Ashby	☐ ▓
Balboa Park	Ocean Ave and San Jose	■ ▓ ▒
Bay Fair	San Leandro & Coelho	☐ ▓
Berkeley	Shattuck Ave and Center	☐ ▓
Civic Center	Market betw 7th & 8th	■ ▓ ▒
Coliseum	San Leandro Hegenberger	☐ ▓
Concord	Clayton Rd & Oakland	■
Daly City	Knowles E Serra Frwy	■ ▓ ▒
El Cerrito del Norte	Key Route Bl Glen Mawr	☐ ▒
El Cerrito Plaza	Key Route Bl Fairmount	☐ ▒
Embarcadero	Main and Market	■ ▓ ▒
Fremont	Mowry and Bart Way	☐ ▓
Fruitvale	San Leandro & Fruitvale	☐ ▓
Glen Park	Bosworth off San Jose	■ ▓ ▒
Hayward	San Leandro Blvd C St	☐ ▓
Lafayette	Deerhill & Happy Valley	■
Lake Merritt	E 8th St and Lakeside Dr	☐ ▓
MacArthur	MacArthur Blvd off Rt.24	☐ ■ ▒
Montgomery	Market and Montgomery	■ ▓ ▒
19th St Oakland	19th and Broadway	☐ ■ ▒
North Berkeley	Sacramento and Delaware	☐ ▒
Oakland City Ctr	12th and Broadway	☐ ■ ▒
Oakland West	5th St and Center St	■ ▓ ▒
Orinda	Camino Pablo & Hwy 24	■
Pleasant Hill	Treat and Wildwood	■
Powell	Market and Powell	■ ▓ ▒
Richmond	MacDonald and 18th St	☐ ▒
Rockridge	Miles and College	■
16th Mission	Mission and 16th St	■ ▓ ▒
San Leandro	San Leandro & Estudillo	☐ ▓
South Hayward	San Leandro Tennyson	☐ ▓
24th Mission	Mission and 24th St	■ ▓ ▒
Union City	Union Sq & Decoto Rd	☐ ▓
Walnut Creek	Ignacio & No. Calif Blvd	■

BUS LINES TO BAY AREA COMMUNITIES

AC TRANSIT TO	GOLDEN GATE TO	SAMTRANS TO
Antioch	Bolinas	Belmont
Berkeley	Corte Madera	Brisbane
Brentwood	Fairfax	Burlingame
Castro Valley	Inverness	Daly City
Crockett	Larkspur	Foster City
El Cerrito	Mill Valley	Half Moon Bay
Emeryville	Muir Woods	Los Altos
Hayward	Novato	Menlo Park
Hercules	Petaluma	Millbrae
Oakland	San Anselmo	Pacifica
Pittsburg	San Rafael	Palo Alto
Richmond	Santa Rosa	Redwood City
Rodeo	Sausalito	San Bruno
San Leandro	Sebastopol	San Mateo
San Pablo	Tiburon	So San Francisco

FOR ADDITIONAL HIGHWAY AND TRANSIT INFORMATION SEE PAGE 79

HOTELS
DOWNTOWN

DOWNTOWN HOTELS—BY MAP NUMBER

1 Howard Johnson	26 Hyatt Regency	50 Four Season Clift
2 Wharf	27 Carlton	51 Hotel Diva
3 Travelodge Fishrmn	28 York	52 Pacific Plaza
4 Travelodge Wharf	29 Commodore	53 Raphael
5 Inn at Fisherman	30 Canterbury	54 St. Francis
6 Holiday Fisherman	31 Beresford	55 King George
7 Sheraton Fisherman	32 Orchard	56 Stewart
8 Marriott	33 Cartwright	57 Hilton SF
9 Ramada Fisherman	34 Holiday Union	59 Handlery
10 Quality	35 Beverly Plaza	60 Manx
11 Cable	36 Inn Union Sq	61 Hotel Union Sq
12 Lombard	36 Kensington Pk	62 Travelodge D'town
13 Rancho Lombard	37 Chancellor	63 Oasis
14 Vagabond	38 Sir Francis	64 Travelodge Civic
15 Pacific Heights	39 Hyatt Union	65 Caravan
16 Washington Square	40 Campton Place	66 Ramada Renaiss
17 Broadway Manor	41 Galleria Park	67 Oxford
18 Castle	42 Sheraton Palace	68 Meridien
19 Holiday Financial	43 Cathedral	69 Merlin
20 Fairmont	44 Lombard	70 San Franciscan
21 Holiday Golden	45 Grosvenor Civic	71 Holiday Civic
22 Huntington	46 Rodeway	72 Best West Flamingo
23 Mark Hopkins	47 El Cortez	73 Best West American
24 Stanford Court	48 Bellevue	74 Best West Civic
25 Vintage	49 Californian	

DOWNTOWN HOTELS—ALPHABETICAL

Hotel (Room Rate*)	Address	Map No	Telephone	Rooms
Bellevue (b)	505 Geary Street	48	474-3600	250
Beresford (b)	635 Sutter Street	31	673-9900	111
Best West Americania (b)	121 7th Street	73	626-0200	145
Best West-Civic Center (c)	364 Ninth Street	74	621-2826	57
Best West-Flamingo Ctr (c)	114 7th Street	72	621-0701	38
Beverly Plaza (c)	342 Grant Ave	35	781-3566	200
Broadway Manor (c)	Van Ness & Broadway	17	776-7900	60
Cable Motor Inn (b)	1450 Lombard Street	11	673-0691	70
Californian (c)	405 Taylor Street	49	885-2500	252
Campton Place (a)	340 Stockton Street	40	781-5555	126
Canterbury/Whitehall (b)	750 Sutter Street	30	474-6464	216
Caravan Lodge (c)	601 Eddy Street	65	776-1380	44
Carlton (c)	1075 Sutter Street	27	673-0242	170
Cartwright (b)	524 Sutter Street	33	421-2865	119
Castle Inn (c)	1565 Broadway	18	441-1155	24
Cathedral Hill (a)	Van Ness & Geary	43	776-8200	403
Chancellor (c)	433 Powell Street	37	362-2004	150
Commodore Internat'l (c)	825 Sutter Street	29	885-2464	150
El Cortez (c)	550 Geary Street	47	775-5000	175
Fairmont Hotel/Tower (a)	California & Mason	20	772-5000	600
Four Seasons Clift (a)	Geary & Taylor	50	775-4700	400
Galleria Park (a)	191 Sutter Street	41	781-3060	177
Grosvenor-Civic Center (b)	1050 Van Ness Avenue	45	673-4711	151
Handlery Motor Inn (a)	260 O'Farrell Street	59	986-2526	95

*ROOM RATES (DOUBLE): (a) $90-200   (b) $65-85   (c) $45-65

HOTELS—ALPHABETICAL (Continued)

Hotel (Room Rate*)	Address	Map No	Telephone	Rooms
Hilton SF Hotel & Tower (a +)	Mason & O'Farrell	57	771-1400	1685
Holiday Inn-Civic Ctr (b)	50 Eighth Street	71	626-6103	400
Holiday Inn Financial Dis (a)	750 Kearny Street	19	433-6600	558
Holiday Fisherman's Wharf (a)	1300 Columbus Ave	6	771-9000	340
Holiday Inn Golden Gate (a)	1500 Van Ness Ave	21	441-4000	500
Holiday Inn Union Sq (a)	480 Sutter Street	34	398-8900	416
Hotel Diva (a +)	440 Geary Street	51	885-0200	125
Hotel Union Square (b)	114 Powell Street	61	397-3000	160
Howard Johnson's (b)	580 Beach Street	1	775-3800	130
Huntington (a +)	1075 California Street	22	474-5400	210
Hyatt on Union Square (a +)	345 Stockton Street	39	398-1234	701
Hyatt Regency S. F. (a +)	5 Embarcadero Center	26	788-1234	840
Inn on Fisherman's (a +)	2655 Hyde Street	5	771-0200	24
Inn on Union Sq, The (a +)	440 Post Street	36	397-3510	27
Kensington Park (a)	450 Post Street	36	788-6400	100
King George (c)	334 Mason Street	55	781-5050	144
Lombard Hotel (b)	1015 Geary Street	44	673-5232	100
Lombard Motor Inn (c)	1475 Lombard Street	12	441-6000	48
Manx (b)	225 Powell Street	60	421-7070	183
Mark Hopkins (a +)	1 Nob Hill	23	392-3434	400
Marriott Fisherman's (a)	1250 Columbus Ave	8	775-7555	256
Meridien (a +)	50 Third Street	68	974-6400	675
Merlin (c)	85 Fifth Street	69	421-7500	180
Oasis Motel (c)	900 Franklin Street	63	885-6865	59
Orchard (b)	562 Sutter Street	32	397-4615	120
Oxford (c)	Mason & Market	67	775-4600	114
Pacific Heights Inn (c)	1555 Union Street	15	776-3310	39
Pacific Plaza (a)	501 Post Street	52	441-7100	140
Quality Inn of S. F. (b)	2775 Van Ness Ave	10	928-5000	140
Ramada Fisherman's (a)	590 Bay Street	9	885-4700	240
Ramada Renaissance (a)	55 Cyril Magnin	66	392-8000	1015
Rancho Lombard (c)	1501 Lombard Street	13	474-3030	34
Raphael, The (b)	386 Geary Street	53	986-2000	150
Rodeway Inn (c)	895 Geary Street	46	441-8220	73
San Franciscan (a)	1231 Market Street	70	626-8000	399
St. Francis (Westin) (a)	Powell & Geary	54	397-7000	1200
Sheraton Fisherman's (a)	2500 Mason Street	7	362-5500	542
Sheraton Palace (a)	639 Market Street	42	392-8600	592
Sir Francis Drake (a)	450 Powell Street	38	392-7755	415
Stanford Court (a +)	California & Powell	24	989-3500	402
Stewart (b)	351 Geary Street	56	781-7800	300
Travelodge-Civic Ctr (c)	655 Ellis Street	64	771-3000	100
Travelodge-D'town S.F. (c)	790 Ellis Street	62	775-7612	81
Travelodge Fisherman's (b)	250 Beach Street	3	392-6700	250
Travelodge Wharf (b)	1201 Columbus Avenue	4	776-7070	24
Vagabond Motor (c)	2550 Van Ness Ave	14	776-7500	134
Vintage Court (b)	650 Bush Street	25	392-4666	106
Washington Square Inn (b +)	1660 Stockton Street	16	981-4220	15
Wharf Motel (b)	2601 Mason Street	2	673-7411	51
York (a)	940 Sutter Street	28	885-6800	100

OTHER ACCOMODATIONS:

American Family B & B	PO Box 349, San Francisco, 94101	931-3083
Bed & Breakfast International	151 Ardmore Rd, Kensington, 94707	525-4569
Distinctive Inns-Wine Country	4350 Barnes Rd, Santa Rosa, 95401	(707) 575-7350

20 *ROOM RATES (DOUBLE): (a) $90-200 (b) $65-85 (c) $45-65

HOTELS WESTERN ADDITION

© FLASHMAPS PUBLICATIONS Inc.

AIRPORT

HOTELS—WESTERN ADDITION

Hotel (Room Rate*)	Address	Map No	Telephone	Rooms
Alfa Inn (c)	2505 Lombard Street	4	921-2505	22
Bed & Breakfast Inn (a)	4 Charlton Court	7	921-9784	9
Capri (b)	2015 Greenwich Avenue	6	346-4667	45
De Ville (c)	2599 Lombard Street	3	346-4664	40
El Drisco (b)	2901 Pacific Avenue	9	346-2880	41
Kyoto Best Western (b)	1800 Sutter Street	12	921-4000	124
Laurel Motor Inn (c)	444 Presidio Avenue	10	567-8467	50
Mansion Hotel (a)	2220 Sacramento Street	11	929-9444	18
Marina (b)	2576 Lombard Street	1	921-9406	45
Miyako (a)	1625 Post Street	14	922-3200	208
Queen Anne Inn (a)	1590 Sutter Street	13	441-2828	49
Sea Captain (c)	2322 Lombard Street	2	921-4980	37
Sherman Inn (a +)	2160 Green Street	8	563-3600	15
Star Motel (c)	1727 Lombard Street	5	346-8250	52

HOTELS—AIRPORT

AMFAC Hotel (a)	1380 Old Bayshore, Burlingame	11	347-5444	320
Airport Executive (b)	275 So. Airport Blvd, SSF	4	873-3550	125
Best West El Rancho (b)	1100 El Camino Real, Millbrae	8	588-2912	200
Best West Grosvenor (b)	380 So. Airport Blvd, SSF	7	873-3200	320
Cavalier (c)	1330 El Camino Real, SSF	1	589-8875	48
Clarion Hotel (a)	401E Millbrae, Millbrae	10	692-6363	223
Dunfey's San Mateo (a)	1770 So. Amphlett, San Mateo	13	573-7661	272
Hilton Inn (a)	S. F. International Airport	9	589-0770	552
Holiday Inn Airport (b)	245 S Airport Blvd, SSF	6	589-7200	332
Holiday Inn Crwn Plz (a)	600 Airport Blvd	7	340-8500	416
Holiday Inn Marine (a)	1101 Shoreway Dr, Belmont	14	591-1471	195
Hyatt Burlingame (a)	1333 Bayshore Hwy Burlingame	12	342-7741	308
Imperial "400" (c)	222 So. Airport Blvd, SSF	3	589-9055	42
Sheraton Inn Airport (b)	1177 Airport Blvd Burlingame	2	342-9200	315
Travelodge Internatl (c)	326 So. Airport Blvd, SSF	5	583-9600	197

*ROOM RATES (DOUBLE): (a) $90-200 (b) $65-85 (c) $45-65 **21**

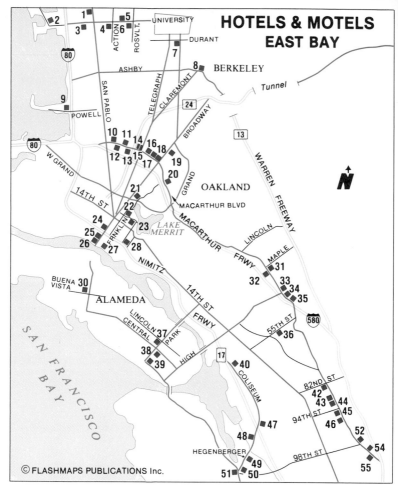

HOTELS & MOTELS — BY MAP NUMBER
ALAMEDA • BERKELEY • OAKLAND

1 Golden Bear	15 M-B Motel	28 Civic Center	44 Mission
2 Marriott	16 Friendship Inn	30 Alameda	45 Sun Crest
3 BW Berkeley	17 Town Lodge	31 Oaks	46 Empire
4 Bel Air	18 Westwind	32 Highlander	47 Holiday Inn
5 Friendship	19 Broadway	33 Holiday	48 Hyatt Oakland
6 Berkeley Travel	20 Motel Five	34 Mills	49 Travel-Oakland
7 Durant	21 Lk Merritt Ldg	35 Sage	50 Edgewater
8 Claremont	23 Lake Merritt	36 Fifty-Fifth	51 Hilton Inn
9 Holiday-Emery	24 Hyatt Regncy	37 Linoaks	52 Beverly Terr
10 Capri	24 London	38 Islander	54 Commodore
11 Palms	25 BW Thundrbd	39 Coral Reef	55 Farm Hse
12 Mosswood	25 Washington	40 Coliseum	
13 Sleepy Hollow	26 BW Boatel	42 Mel-Rey	
14 Rio Motel	27 Jack London	43 Cactus	

22

HOTELS & MOTELS—ALPHABETICAL
ALAMEDA • BERKELEY • OAKLAND

Hotel	Address	Map No.	Telephone	Rooms
Alameda Royal	1925 Webster Ave	30	521-8400	52
Bel Air Motel Apts	1330 Univ Ave	4	848-8061	36
Berkeley Travelodge	1820 University Ave	6	843-4262	30
Best West-Berkeley Hse	920 University	3	849-1121	112
Best West-Boatel Lodge	21 Jack London Sq	26	836-3800	70
Best West-Thunderbird	233 Broadway	25	452-4565	103
Beverly Terrace	9920 MacArthur Blvd	52	569-6946	20
Broadway	4140 Broadway	19	653-0458	26
Cactus Hotel	9029 MacArthur Blvd	43	632-7183	31
Capri Motel	722 W MacArthur Blvd	10	658-0465	31
Civic Center Lodge	6th & Fallon	28	444-4139	32
Claremont Resort	Claremont Ave & Ashby	8	843-3000	230
Coliseum	4801 Coliseum Way	40	532-4084	36
Commodore	10100 MacArthur Blvd	54	568-4068	13
Coral Reef	400 Park	39	521-2330	96
Durant Hotel	2600 Durant Ave	7	845-8981	140
Edgewater West	10 Hegenberger Rd	50	632-6262	350
Empire	9451 MacArthur Blvd	46	636-0210	22
Farm House	10451 MacArthur Blvd	55	638-4021	15
Fifty-Fifth Ave	2320 55th Ave	36	536-2021	30
Friendship Inn	490 W MacArthur Blvd	16	653-4225	50
Friendship Motel	1619 University Ave	5	841-3844	23
Golden Bear	1620 San Pablo Ave	1	525-6770	42
Highlander	3255 MacArthur Blvd	32	482-3031	26
Hilton Inn	Oakland Internat'l Airport	51	635-5000	300
Holiday Inn Bay Brdg	1800 Powell, Emeryville	9	658-9300	281
Holiday Inn-Oak. Airport	Nimitz Frwy & Hegenberger	47	562-5311	200
Holiday Motel	4474 MacArthur Blvd	33	530-2700	24
Hyatt Oakland	455 Hegenberger Rd	48	562-6100	350
Hyatt Regency	1001 Broadway	24	893-1234	488
Islander Lodge	2428 Central Ave	38	865-2121	62
Jack London Inn	444 Embarcadero West	27	444-2032	148
Lake Merritt	1800 Madison	23	832-2300	49
Lake Merritt Lodge	2332 Harrison	21	893-3130	140
Linoaks	2310 Lincoln Ave	37	523-6633	50
London Lodge	Broadway & 7th St	24	451-6316	200
M-B Motel	430 W MacArthur Blvd	15	652-2538	20
Marriott Berkeley Marina	200 Marina Blvd	2	548-7920	241
Mel-Rey Motel	8314 MacArthur Blvd	42	638-8433	15
Mills	4550 MacArthur Blvd	34	530-0651	23
Mission	9235 MacArthur Blvd	44	632-5513	17
Mosswood	683 W MacArthur Blvd	12	655-5817	28
Motel Five	55 MacArthur Blvd	20	653-5959	45
Oaks Motel	3250 MacArthur Blvd	31	482-3200	29
Palms Motel	829 W MacArthur Blvd	11	655-0563	19
Rio Motel	526 W MacArthur Blvd	14	654-2008	17
Sage Motel	4844 MacArthur Blvd	35	530-0800	18
Sleepy Hollow	544 W MacArthur Blvd	13	655-4796	27
Sun Crest	9410 MacArthur Blvd	45	562-5203	18
Town Lodge	370 W MacArthur Blvd	17	654-3940	17
Travelodge-Oak Airport	150 Hegenberger Rd	49	635-5300	200
Washington Inn	495 Tenth Street	25	495-1776	48
Westwind Lodge	336 W MacArthur Blvd	18	654-1235	28

AVERAGE ROOM RATE $45 · $85   LUXURY ACCOMODATIONS $85 · $175

RESTAURANTS
DOWNTOWN

DOWNTOWN RESTAURANTS—BY MAP NUMBER
(See index for other listings)

1 Giglio	59 Hippo	105 Vasilis
2 El Tapatio	60 Harris	106 Plaza
3 Chez Marguerite	61 Cherry Flower	106 One Up
4 Gelco's	62 Ernie's	107 Hoffman's Grill
6 Julius Castle	63 Tao-Tao	108 Hilltop Room
7 Mama's Wash Sq	64 House Prime Rib	108 Tommy's Joynt
8 Shadows	65 Le Tournesol	109 Nero's
10 La Contadina	66 Le Club	110 Post Street
11 Washington Square	67 Zola's	110 Tiki Bob's
12 Beethoven	68 Scoma's Pyramid	111 David's Deli
13 Amelio's	69 Canlis'	112 Salmagundi
14 Capp's Corner	69 Squire	113 New Joe's
16 Fior d'Italia	69 Crown Room	113 Pam Pam East
17 La Felce	70 Jacks	114 English Grill
18 Gold Spike	71 Swan Oyster Depot	114 Victor's
19 North Beach	72 Mama's of SF	115 Mayfair
20 Caffe Sport	73 L'Etoile	116 Iron Horse
22 Savoy-Tivoli	73 Big Four	118 Swiss Alps
23 Old Spaghetti Factry	74 Alexis	119 La Mere Duquesne
24 Casablanca	75 Nob Hill	120 French Room
26 Xenios	75 Vienna Coffee	121 Marrakech
28 North China	76 Fournou's	122 La Bourgogne
29 Szechwan	77 Victor's	123 Christophe
30 Sorrento	78 Nikko Sukiyaki	124 Le Trianon
32 Pasha	79 Cafe Mozart	125 Omar Khayyam's
33 Alfred's	80 L'Orangerie	127 Chef's Table
34 Restaurant France	81 Masa's	127 Gazebo
36 Des Alpes	82 Sam's Grill	127 Phil Lehr's
37 Adolph's	83 Graziano's	127 Henri's
38 Basta Pasta	84 Piero's	128 Bardelli's
39 La Pantera	86 Maye's Oyster	129 Union Pacific
40 Luigi's	87 Lehr's Greenhouse	130 Chez Leon
41 Guido's	89 Sutter 500	131 John's Grill
42 Little Joe	90 Le Chambord	132 Pierre at Meridien
43 Basque Hotel	91 White Elephant	133 Original Joe's
44 Enrico's	92 Caravansary	134 Corintia
45 Vanessi's	93 Claude's	134 Polo's
46 Hunan	93 Midori	134 Veranda, The
47 Elu's	94 Le Central	135 Athens
48 La Mirabelle	95 Kinokawa	136 Joe Jung's
49 Taj of India	95 Orsi	137 Palm Garden
50 Columbus Italian	96 Fleur de Lys	138 Kundan
51 Cafe Americain	97 Trader Vic's	138 Modesto
52 Greek Taverna	98 La Quiche	139 Stars
53 Tommaso's	99 White Horse	140 Kimball's
54 Cho Cho	100 Donatello	141 Ivy's
55 Mabuhay	101 Sears	142 Hayes St
56 St. Pierre	102 Drake's Tavern	143 Raffles
57 434 Pacific Ave	103 Campton Place	144 Le Vaudeville
58 Jovanelo's	104 Magic Pan	145 Rooney's at Mart

ALPHABETICAL LISTINGS ON PAGES 26, 27, 28.

DOWNTOWN RESTAURANTS—ALPHABETICAL

Restaurant	Address	Map No.	Cuisine	Average Dinner Price ★	Telephone
Adolph's	641 Vallejo St	37	Italian	$15-20	392-6333
Alexis	1001 California St	74	French	20+	885-6400
Alfred's	886 Broadway	33	Italian	10-15	781-7058
Amelio's	1630 Powell St	13	North Ital	20-25	397-4339
Athens	39 Mason St	135	Greek	7-9	775-1929
Bardelli's	243 O'Farrell St	128	Italian	10-20	982-0243
Basque	15 Romolo Pl	43	French	6-10	788-9404
Basta Pasta	1268 Grant St	38	Italian	15-25	434-2248
Beethoven	1701 Powell	12	German	15-20	391-4488
Big Four	1075 California St	73	Continental	25-30	771-1140
Cafe Americain	317 Columbus Av	51	Amer/Sfd	15-20	981-8266
Cafe Mozart	708 Bush St	79	Continental	35+	391-8480
Caffe Sport	574 Green St	20	Italian	4-9	981-1251
Campton Place	Campton Pl Htl	103	American	25+	781-5555
Canlis'	Fairmont Hotel	69	American	35+	392-0113
Capp's Corner	1600 Powell St	14	American	9-14	989-2589
Caravansary	310 Sutter St	92	Mid East	10-15	362-4640
Casablanca	2323 Polk St	24	Continental	10-20	441-2244
Chef's Table	SF Hilton Htl	127	Continental	25+	771-1400
Cherry Flower	124 Columbus Av	61	Vietnamese	8-13	398-9101
Chez Leon	124 Ellis St	130	French	15-20	982-1093
Chez Marguerite	2330 Taylor St	3	French	10-20	775-9785
Cho Cho	1020 Kearney St	54	Japanese	9-13	397-3066
Christophe	320 Mason St	123	French	9-15	433-7560
Claude's	334 Grant Ave	93	French	10-15	788-6262
Columbus Italian	611 Broadway	50	Italian	5-10	781-2939
Corintia	Ramada Ren. Htl	134	North Ital	25-30	392-8000
Crown Room	Fairmont Hotel	69	Continental	25-35	772-5131
David's Deli	474 Geary St	111	Kosher	10-20	771-1600
Des Alpes	732 Broadway	36	Basque	10-15	788-9900
Donatello	Pacific Plaza Htl	100	Italian	25-35	441-7182
Drake's Tavern	Francis Drake Htl	102	English	10-15	392-7755
El Tapatio	475 Francisco St	2	Mexican	9-15	981-3018
Elu's	787 Broadway	47	Basque	5-10	781-7287
English Grill	Mark Hopkins Htl	114	Seafood	15-20	397-7000
Enrico's Sidewlk Cafe	504 Broadway	44	Italian	9-13	392-6220
Ernie's	847 Montgomery	62	French	40+	397-5969
Fior d'Italia	601 Union St	16	Italian	15-20	986-1886
Fleur de Lys	777 Sutter St	96	French	15-20	673-7779
434 Pacific Ave	434 Pacific Ave	57	Japanese	8-14	397-3265
Fournou's Ovens	Stanford Court Htl	76	Continental	30+	989-1910
French Room	Four Seas Clift Htl	120	Continental	35+	775-4700
Gazebo	SF Hilton Htl	127	Continental	15-25	771-1400
Gelco's	1450 Lombard St	4	Balkan	15-20	928-1054
Giglio	545 Francisco St	1	Italian	15-20	441-1040
Gold Spike	527 Columbus Av	18	American	12-18	986-9747
Graziano's	453 Pine St	83	Italian	15-20	981-4800
Greek Taverna	256 Columbus Av	52	Greek	10-15	362-7260
Guido's	347 Columbus Av	41	North Ital	12-20	982-2157
Harris Steak	2100 Van Ness	60	American	20-25	673-1888

26

★ *Prices do not include drinks or gratuities*

DOWNTOWN RESTAURANTS—ALPHABETICAL

Restaurant	Address	Map No.	Cuisine	Average Dinner Price ★	Telephone
Hayes St Grill	320 Hayes St	142	Seafood	10-15	863-5545
Henri's Room at Top	SF Hilton Htl	127	Continental	20-25	771-1400
Hilltop Room	Cathedral Hill Htl	108	Continental	15-20	776-8200
Hippo, The	Van Ness/Pacific	59	American	7-10	771-3939
Hoffman's Grill	619 Market	107	American	10-16	421-1467
House Prime Rib	1906 Van Ness Av	64	American	15-20	885-4605
Hunan	924 Sansome St	46	Chinese	10-15	956-7727
Iron Horse	19 Maiden Lane	116	Continental	20-25	362-8133
Ivy's	398 Hayes St	141	American	15-20	626-3930
Jack's	615 Sacramento	70	French	15-20	986-9854
Joe Jung's	891 Market	136	Chin/Amer	9-15	362-6706
John's Grill	63 Ellis St	131	American	15-20	986-0069
Jovanelo's	840 Sansome St	58	Italian	15-20	986-8050
Julius Castle	1541 Montgomery	6	North Ital	20-25	362-3042
Kimball's	300 Grove Street	140	Continental	15-20	861-5555
Kinokawa	347 Grant Avenue	95	Japanese	10-15	956-6085
Kundan	601 Van Ness	138	Indian	20-25	673-5600
L'Etoile	1075 California St	73	French	20-25	771-1529
L'Orangerie	1540 Polk St	80	French	25+	776-9570
La Bourgogne	330 Mason St	122	French	20-25	362-7352
La Contandina	1800 Mason St	10	French	9-15	982-5728
La Felce	1570 Stockton St	17	Italian	9-14	392-8321
La Mere Duquesne	101 Shannon Alley	119	French	15-20	776-7600
La Mirabelle	1326 Powell St	48	French	25+	421-3374
La Pantera Cafe	1234 Grant Ave	39	Italian	10-15	392-0170
La Quiche	550 Taylor St	98	Creperie	8-13	441-2711
Le Central	453 Bush St	94	French	10-15	391-2233
Le Club	Clay & Jones Sts	66	French	15-20	771-5400
Le Chambord	152 Kearney	90	French	15-20	434-3688
Le Tournesol	1760 Polk St	65	Natural Fd	9-14	441-1760
Le Trianon R. Verdon	242 O'Farrell	124	Continental	30+	982-9353
Le Vaudeville	41 Grove Street	144	French	20-25	861-0788
Lehr's Greenhouse	750 Sutter St	87	American	10-15	474-6478
Little Joe's	523 Broadway	42	Italian	5-8	982-7639
Luigi's	353 Columbus Av	40	Italian	6-9	397-1697
Mabuhay Gardens	443 Broadway	55	Philippine	5-10	956-3315
Magic Pan	341 Sutter St	104	Creperie	8-11	788-7397
Mama's of SF	1177 California St	72	American	10-15	928-1004
Mama's Washngtn Sq	1701 Stockton St	7	American	9-14	362-6421
Marrakech	419 O'Farrell St	121	Moroccan	20-25	776-6717
Masa's	Vintage Court Htl	81	Continental	35-40	989-7154
Maye's Oyster Hse	1233 Polk St	86	Seafood	15-19	474-7674
Mayfair	116 Maiden Lane	115	American	20-25	421-1093
Midori	352 Grant Ave	93	Japanese	6-10	982-3546
Modesto Lanzone's	601 Van Ness	138	Italian	20-25	928-0400
Nero's	712 Geary St	109	Italian	10-15	673-3903
New Joe's	347 Geary St	113	Italian	10-16	989-6733
Nikko Sukiyaki	1450 Van Ness	78	Japanese	9-15	474-7722
Nob Hill	Mark Hopkins Htl	75	Continental	30+	392-3434
North Beach	1512 Stockton	19	North Ital	10-15	392-1587

★ Prices do not include drinks or gratuities

DOWNTOWN RESTAURANTS—ALPHABETICAL

Restaurant	Address	Map No.	Cuisine	Average Dinner Price ★	Telephone
North China	2315 Van Ness	28	Chinese	$9-13	673-8201
Old Spaghetti Factory	478 Green St	23	Italian	7-12	776-2511
Omar Khayyam's	196 O'Farrell St	125	Armenian	15-20	781-1010
One Up	Hyatt-Union Sq	106	Continental	25+	398-1234
Original Joe's	144 Taylor St	133	Italian	10-15	775-4877
Orsi	375 Bush St	95	North Ital	25+	981-6535
Palm Garden Grill	975 Market St	137	Germ/Sfd	12-15	821-6005
Pam Pam East	398 Geary St	113	American	7-10	433-0113
Pasha	1516 Broadway	32	Mid East	15-20	885-4477
Phil Lehr's Steakery	Hilton Hotel	127	American	15-20	673-6800
Pierre at Meridien	Meridien Hotel	132	Continental	40+	974-6400
Piero's	447 Pine St	84	Italian	9-13	421-7104
Plaza	Hyatt-Union Sq	106	American	15-20	398-1234
Polo's	34 Mason St	134	Italian	7-10	362-7719
Post Street	632 Post St	110	Continental	9-12	928-9934
Raffles	1390 Market St	143	Polynesian	9-15	621-8601
Restaurant de France	780 Broadway	34	French	15-20	421-5541
Rooney's at the Mart	32 9th Street	145	Continental	15-20	861-2820
Salmagundi	442 Geary St	112	Soup/Quiche	6-10	441-0894
Sam's Grill	374 Bush St	82	Seafood	15-20	421-0594
Savoy-Tivoli	1434 Grant Ave	22	Continental	6-10	362-7023
Scoma's by Pyramid	565 Clay St	68	Seafood	20-25	434-2345
Sears	439 Powell St	101	American	6-10	986-1160
Shadows, The	1349 Montgomery	8	Ger/Amer	10-15	982-5536
Sorrento	2141 Polk St	30	Italian	10-14	474-0422
Squire Room	Fairmont Hotel	69	American	30+	772-5211
St Pierre	580 Pacific Ave	56	French	20-25	397-5538
Stars	150 Redwood	139	French	20-30	861-7827
Sutter 500	500 Sutter St	89	French	10-15	362-3346
Swan Oyster Depot	1517 Polk St	71	American	10-14	673-1101
Swiss Alps	605 Post St	118	Swiss	10-15	885-0947
Szechwan	2209 Polk St	29	Chinese	15-20	474-8282
Taj of India	825 Pacific Ave	49	Indian	15-20	392-0089
Tao-Tao	675 Jackson	63	Cantonese	11-15	982-6125
Tiki Bob's	599 Post St	110	Polynesian	20-25	673-7500
Tommaso's	1042 Kearny St	53	Italian	9-13	398-9696
Tommy's Joynt	Van Ness & Geary	108	American	7-10	775-4216
Trader Vic's	20 Cosmo Place	97	Polynesian	20-25	776-2232
Union Pacific	160 Ellis St	129	California	12-18	397-8470
Vanessi's	498 Broadway	45	Italian	10-20	421-0890
Vasilis	44 Campton Place	105	Continental	15-20	392-5373
Veranda, The	Ramada Renaiss	134	California	15-20	392-8000
Victor's Restaurant	St Francis Tower	114	Continental	35+	956-7777
Victor's Pizza	1411 Polk St	77	Italian	5-8	885-1660
Vienna Coffee House	Mark Hopkins Htl	75	American	10-15	392-3434
Washington Square	1707 Powell St	11	Italian	10-15	982-8123
White Elephant	Holiday-Union Sq	91	Continental	14-18	398-1331
White Horse	637 Sutter St	99	Continental	7-11	771-1708
Xenios	2237 Polk St	26	Greek	9-14	775-2800
Zola's	1722 Sacramento	67	French	15-20	775-3311

★ *Prices do not include drinks or gratuities*

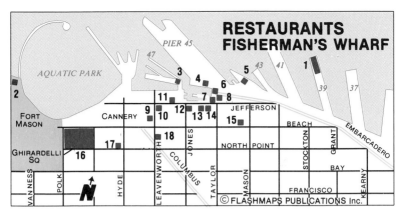

RESTAURANTS FISHERMAN'S WHARF

1 Swiss Louis
1 Vannelli's
1 Pepe's on Pier
1 Chic's Pl/Neptune
1 Old Swiss House
1 Nakamura
2 Greens-Fort Mason
3 Scoma's
4 Sabella La Torre
5 Franciscan

6 Alioto's
7 Tarantino's
8 A. Sabella's
9 El Greco
9 Chart House
9 Las Margaritas
9 Shang Yuen
10 Houlihan's
11 Pompei's Grotto
12 Castagnola

13 DiMaggio's
14 Tokyo Sukiyaki
15 Tandoori
16 Gaylord India
16 Modesto Lanzone's
16 Maxwell's Plum
16 Mandarin, The
16 Paprikas Fono
17 Chez Michel
18 Charlie's Conservatry

CANNERY-FISHERMAN'S WHARF-GHIRARDELLI

Restaurant	Address	Map No.	Cuisine	Average Price ★	Telephone
A. Sabella's	2766 Taylor St	4	Seafood	$10-15	771-6775
Alioto's	Fisherman's Wharf	6	Seafood	10-25	673-0183
Castagnola	Jefferson & Jones	12	Seafood	10-15	775-5015
Charlie's Conservtry	2750 Leavenworth	18	Seafood	10-20	776-8511
Chart House	The Cannery	9	Stk/Seafd	12-18	474-3476
Chez Michel	804 North Point	17	French	20-25	771-6077
Chic's Place	Pier 39	1	Seafood	10-20	421-2442
DiMaggio's	247 Jefferson St	13	Seafood	10-15	673-2266
El Greco	The Cannery	9	Spanish	7-9	771-0410
Franciscan	Pier 43 ½ Embarc	5	Seafood	10-15	362-7733
Gaylord India	Ghirardelli Square	16	Indian	15-20	771-8822
Greens	Fort Mason	2	Natural Fds	15-20	771-6222
Houlihan's	2800 Leavenworth	10	Stk/Seafd	10-17	775-7523
Las Margaritas	The Cannery	9	Mexican	10-15	776-6996
Mandarin	Ghirardelli Square	16	Chinese	10-20	673-8812
Maxwell's Plum	Ghirardelli Square	16	Continental	10-20	441-4140
Modesto Lanzone's	Ghirardelli Square	16	Italian	25+	771-2880
Nakamura	Pier 39	1	Japanese	10-16	421-6818
Neptune's Palace	Pier 39	1	Seafood	10-15	434-2260
Old Swiss House	Pier 39	1	Swiss	10-20	434-0432
Paprikas Fono	Ghirardelli Square	16	Hungarian	10-20	441-1223
Pepe's on Pier	Pier 39	1	Mexican	5-9	434-1818
Pompei's Grotto	340 Jefferson	11	Seafood	8-13	776-9265
Sabella & La Torre	No. 3 Fisherman's	4	Seafood	10-15	673-2824
Scoma's	Pier 47 Fishermans	3	Seafood	10-15	771-4383
Shang Yuen	The Cannery	9	Chinese	10-20	771-4200
Swiss Louis	Pier 39	1	Italian	10-20	421-2913
Tandoori	420 Beach St	15	Indian	10-15	778-6366
Tarantino's	206 Jefferson St	7	Seafood	10-20	775-5600
Tokyo Sukiyaki	225 Jefferson St	14	Japanese	10-15	775-9030
Vannelli's	Pier 39	1	Seafood	10-15	421-7261

★ Prices do not include drinks or gratuities.

29

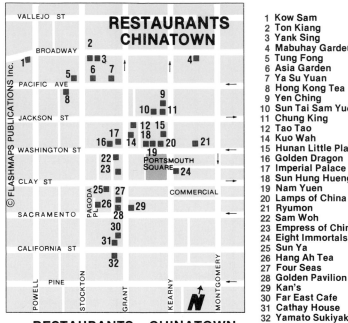

RESTAURANTS CHINATOWN

1 Kow Sam
2 Ton Kiang
3 Yank Sing
4 Mabuhay Gardens
5 Tung Fong
6 Asia Garden
7 Ya Su Yuan
8 Hong Kong Tea
9 Yen Ching
10 Sun Tai Sam Yuen
11 Chung King
12 Tao Tao
14 Kuo Wah
15 Hunan Little Place
16 Golden Dragon
17 Imperial Palace
18 Sun Hung Hueng
19 Nam Yuen
20 Lamps of China
21 Ryumon
22 Sam Woh
23 Empress of China
24 Eight Immortals
25 Sun Ya
26 Hang Ah Tea
27 Four Seas
28 Golden Pavilion
29 Kan's
30 Far East Cafe
31 Cathay House
32 Yamato Sukiyaki

RESTAURANTS—CHINATOWN

Restaurant	Address	Map No.	Cuisine	Average Price ★	Telephone
Asia Garden	772 Pacific Ave	6	Cantonese	$6-9	398-5112
Cathay House	718 California St	31	Chinese	10-15	982-3388
Chung King	606 Jackson St	11	Chinese	5-8	986-3899
Eight Immortals	750 Kearny St	24	Chinese	10-15	433-6600
Empress of China	838 Grant Ave	23	Chinese	10-20	434-1345
Far East Cafe	631 Grant Ave	30	Cantonese	7-10	982-3245
Four Seas	731 Grant Ave	27	Chinese	9-14	397-5577
Golden Dragon	822 Washington St	16	Chinese	12-20	398-3920
Golden Pavilion	800 Sacramento St	28	Chinese	12-15	392-2334
Hang Ah Tea Rm	1 Pagoda Place	26	Chinese	6-10	982-5686
Hong Kong Tea	835 Pacific Ave	8	Chinese	5-9	391-6365
Hunan-Little Place	853 Kearney St	15	Chinese	5-9	788-2234
Imperial Palace	919 Grant Ave	17	Chinese	15-25	982-4440
Kan's Chinese	708 Grant Ave	29	Chinese	15-20	982-2388
Kow Sam Teahouse	801 Broadway	1	Chinese	6-9	781-6640
Kuo Wah	950 Grant Ave	14	Chinese	9-15	982-1851
Lamps of China	728 Washington	20	Chinese	9-13	989-4400
Mabuhay Gardens	443 Broadway	4	Philippine	6-9	956-3315
Nam Yuen	740 Washington St	19	Cantonese	11-15	781-5636
Ryumon	646 Washington St	21	Mandarin	10-15	421-3868
Sam Woh	813 Washington St	22	Chinese	5-8	982-0596
Sun Hung Hueng	744 Washington St	18	Cantonese	5-9	982-2319
Sun Tai Sam Yuen	622 Jackson St	10	Cantonese	8-12	982-2844
Sun Ya	823 Clay St	25	Chinese	5-9	982-0922
Tao Tao	675 Jackson St	12	Cantonese	9-13	982-6125
Ton Kiang	683 Broadway	2	Chinese	5-8	421-2015
Tung Fong	808 Pacific Ave	5	Chinese	5-9	362-7115
Yamato Sukiyaki	717 California St	32	Japanese	9-14	397-3456
Ya Su Yuan	638 Pacific Ave	7	No Chinese	5-9	986-7386
Yank Sing	671 Broadway	3	Chinese	5-9	781-1111
Yen Ching	939 Kearny St	9	No Chinese	4-8	397-3543

★ Prices do not include drinks or gratuities.

RESTAURANTS—EMBARCADERO / FINANCIAL AREA

Restaurant	Address	Map No.	Cuisine	Average Price ★	Telephone
Bentley's	185 Sutter St	23	Seafood	15-25	989-6895
Blue Fox	659 Merchant St	8	Continental	20 +	981-1177
Calif Culinary Aca	215 Fremont St	25	Continental	10-20	543-2764
Carnelian Room	555 California St	16	Continental	25-30	433-7500
Ciao	230 Jackson St	4	No Italian	15-20	982-9500
Conference Room	50 California St	19	Continental	8-16	398-3722
Doro's	714 Montgomery	6	Continental	25-30	397-6822
Enzo's	Three Embarcadero	13	No Italian	10-18	981-5530
Equinox	Hyatt Regency	15	Continental	20-25	788-1234
Fujiya	One Embarcadero	11	Japanese	8-18	398-1151
Garden Court	Sheraton Palace Htl	24	Continental	10-15	392-8600
Gaylord India	One Embarcadero	11	Indian	8-13	397-7775
Golden Eagle	Four Embarcadero	13	Continental	14-19	982-8831
Hugo's	Hyatt Regency	15	Continental	25 +	788-1234
India House	350 Jackson St	3	Indian	8-14	392-0744
Iron Pot	441 Washington St	10	Italian	8-15	392-2100
L'Olivier	465 Davis Street	5	French	14-20	981-7824
La Fuente	Two Embarcadero	12	Mexican	8-15	982-3363
Lily's	Four Embarcadero	14	Continental	25-35	398-3434
MacArthur Park	607 Front St	2	American	10-15	398-5700
Market Place, The	Hyatt Regency	15	American	10-15	788-1234
Old Poodle Dog	Crocker Galleria	23	French	25 +	392-0353
Orient Express	50 Steuart Place	22	Continental	15-25	957-1776
Paoli's	565 Commercial St	17	Ital/French	15-25	781-7115
Schroeder's Cafe	240 Front St	21	German	5-10	421-4778
Scott's Seafood	Three Embarcadero	13	Seafood	8-15	981-0622
Sinbad's Pier 2	Pier 2	9	Seafood	10-15	781-2555
Square One	170 Pacific Ave	7	American	12-18	788-1110
Tadich Grill	240 California	18	Seafd/Amer	15-25	391-2373
Waterfront Pier 7	Ferry Building	1	Seafood	5-10	391-2696

★ Prices do not include drinks or gratuities

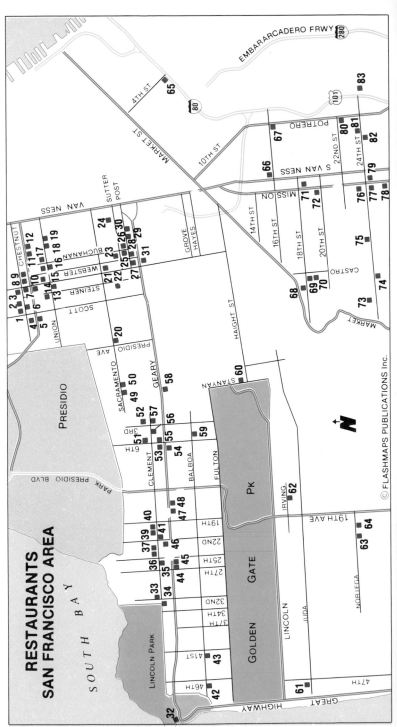

RESTAURANTS
SAN FRANCISCO AREA

© FLASHMAPS PUBLICATIONS Inc.

32

SAN FRANCISCO AREA RESTAURANTS—BY MAP NO

1 Judy's
2 Courtyard, The
3 La Pergola
4 Vlasta's
4 Marina Cafe
6 Caravansary
7 Romano's
8 Luciano
9 Monroe's
10 Balboa Cafe
11 Ronaynes
12 Blue Boar
13 Archil's
14 Lipizzaner
14 Yoshida Ya
15 Prego
16 Jalapenos
16 L'Entrecote
17 Perry's
18 Pasand
19 L'Escargot
20 Le Castel
21 Osome
21 Tora Ya
22 Eichelbaum & Co
23 Otafuku Tei
24 Robert
25 Sanppo
26 Korea House
27 Mitoya

28 Benihana
28 Mifune
28 Misono
29 Akasaka
30 Bamboo Grove
31 Sanpei
32 Cliff House
33 Lung Fung
34 El Mansour
35 Le Beaujolais
36 China Garden
36 Kum Moon
37 Yet Wah
39 Alejandro's
40 Vegi-Food
41 Einer's
42 Mamounia
43 Grapeleaf
44 Tai Ho
45 Kirin
46 El Sombrero
46 Khan Toke
47 Russian Ren
48 Mike's Chinese
49 Magic Flute
50 Mary Gulli's
51 Fountain Court
52 Le St Tropez
53 Cafe Riggio
54 Le Tricolor

55 Le Cyrano
56 A Bit of Indonesia
56 Golden Turtle
57 Garden House
58 Carlos 'n Panchos
59 Harbin
60 Hog Heaven
61 Thanh Long
62 Sagami-Ya
63 Luzern
64 Tien Fu
65 Ruby's
66 Cuba
67 Il Pirata
68 Fanny's
69 Neon Chicken
70 Patio Cafe
71 Coatepeque
72 Bruno's
73 Diamond Sutra
74 Little Italy
75 Matsuya
76 El Zarape
77 La Taqueria
78 Nicaragua
79 La Traviata
80 Aux Delices
81 La Palma
82 La Victoria
83 Noe Valley

SAN FRANCISCO AREA RESTAURANTS

Restaurant	Address	Map No.	Cuisine	Average Dinner Price ★	Telephone
A Bit of Indonesia	211 Clement St	56	Indonesian	$9-14	752-4042
Akasaka	1723 Buchanan	29	Japanese	12-18	921-5360
Alejandro's	1840 Clement St	39	Span/Mex	10-15	668-1184
Archil's	3011 Steiner St	13	Hungarian	9-15	921-2141
Aux Delices	1002 Potrero St	80	Vietnamese	8-12	285-3196
Balboa Cafe	3199 Fillmore St	10	Seafood	20-25	921-3944
Bamboo Grove	Miyako Hotel	30	Jap/Contl	25+	921-5360
Benihana of Tokyo	1737 Post	28	Japanese	10-15	771-8414
Blue Boar Inn	1713 Lombard St	12	English	25+	567-8424
Bruno's	2389 Mission St	72	Continental	9-13	824-2258
Cafe Riggio	4112 Geary Blvd	53	Italian	9-15	221-2114
Caravansary	2263 Chestnut St	6	Mid Eastern	9-13	921-3466
Carlo's 'n Pancho's	3565 Geary St	58	Mexican	10-15	751-5090
China Garden	2110 Clement St	36	No Chinese	9-13	668-9599
Cliff House Upstairs	1090 Point Lobos Rd	32	American	8-14	386-3330
Courtyard, The	2436 Clement St	2	Spanish	9-14	387-7616
Coatepeque	2240 Mission St	71	So American	5-8	863-5237
Cuba	2886 16th St	66	Spanish	6-9	864-9871
Diamond Sutra	737 Diamond St	73	Vegetarian	6-10	285-6988
Eichelbaum & Co	2417 California	22	Varied	10-18	929-9030
Einer's Danish House	1901 Clement St	41	Danish	8-15	386-9860

★ Prices do not include drinks or gratuities

SAN FRANCISCO AREA RESTAURANTS Continued

Restaurant	Address	Map No.	Cuisine	Average Dinner Price ★	Telephone
El Mansour	3123 Clement St	34	Moroccan	$15-18	751-2312
El Sombrero	5800 Geary Blvd	46	Mexican	6-10	221-2382
El Zarape Room	3349 23rd St	76	Mexican	9-14	282-1168
Fanny's	4230 Eighteenth St	68	American	9-13	621-5570
Fountain Court	354 Clement St	51	Chinese	14.95	668-1100
Garden House	133 Clement St	57	Thai	9-12	221-3655
Golden Turtle	308 Fifth Ave	56	Vietnamese	9-15	221-5285
Grapeleaf	4031 Balboa St	43	Lebanese	6-13	668-1515
Harbin Manchurian	327 Balboa St	59	No Chinese	9-14	387-0274
Hog Heaven BBQ	770 Stanyan St	60	Barbecue	5-13	668-2038
Il Pirata	2007 16th St	67	Italian	9-14	626-1845
Jalapenos Mexican	2033 Union St	16	Mexican	6-10	921-2210
Judy's	2268 Chestnut St	1	Continental	12-18	922-4588
Khan Toke	5937 Geary Blvd	46	Chinese	9-14	668-6654
Kirin	6135 Geary Blvd	45	Szechuan	9-12	752-2412
Korea House	1640 Post St	26	Korean	5-9	563-1388
Kum Moon	2109 Clement St	36	Chinese	5-10	221-5656
L'Entrecote de Paris	2032 Union St	16	French	25+	931-5006
L'Escargot	1809 Union St	19	French	15-25	567-0222
La Palma	2884 24th St	81	Mexican	5-10	647-1500
La Pergola	2060 Chestnut St	3	Italian	15-20	563-4500
La Taqueria	2889 Mission St	77	Span/Mex	5-10	285-7117
La Traviata	2854 Mission St	79	Italian	15-20	282-0500
La Victoria Bakery	2937 24th St	82	Spanish	4-8	550-9292
Le Beaujolais	2415 Clement St	35	French	15-20	752-3921
Le Castel	3225 Sacramento	20	French	15-25	921-7115
Le Cyrano	4134 Geary Blvd	55	French	9-13	387-1090
Le St Tropez	126 Clement St	52	French	12-20	347-0408
Le Tricolor	4233 Geary Blvd	54	French	10-15	752-9974
Lipizzaner	2223 Union St	14	Viennese	20-30	921-3424
Little Italy	4109 24th St	74	Italian	10-18	821-1515
Luciano	2018 Lombard St	8	Continental	10-20	922-1900
Lung Fung	3038 Clement St	33	Chinese	4-8	668-3038
Luzern	1431 Noriega St	63	Swiss	9-12	664-2353
Magic Flute	3673 Sacramento	49	Creole/Cajun	8-15	922-1225
Mamounia	4411 Balboa St	42	Moroccan	25+	752-6566
Marina Cafe	2417 Lombard St	5	Ital Seafd	12-18	929-7241
Mary Gulli's	3661 Sacramento	50	Continental	15-25	931-5151
Matsuya	3856 24th St	75	Japanese	6-9	282-7989
Mifune	1737 Post St	28	Japanese	5-10	922-0337
Mike's Chinese Cuisine	5145 Geary Blvd	48	Cantonese	5-8	752-0120
Misono	1737 Post St	28	Japanese	9-15	922-2728
Mitoya	1855 Post St	27	Japanese	9-14	563-2156
Monroe's	1968 Lombard St	9	English	10-15	567-4550
Neon Chicken,The	4063 Eighteenth St	69	American	8-13	863-0484
Nicaragua	3015 Mission St	78	Nicaraguan	6-9	826-3672
Noe Valley Bar Grill	3945 24th St	83	American	9-13	282-9502
Osome	1923 Fillmore St	21	Japanese	9-13	346-2311
Otafuku Tei	1737 Buchanan St	23	Japanese	5-9	931-1578
Pasand	1875 Union St	18	Indian	8-13	922-4498
Patio Cafe	531 Castro St	70	American	6-9	621-4640
Perry's	1944 Union St	17	Continental	15-20	922-9022

★ *Prices do not include drinks or gratuities.*

34

AREA RESTAURANTS—ALPHABETICAL

Restaurant	Address	Map No.	Cuisine	Average Price ★	Telephone
Prego	2000 Union St	15	North Ital	$10-15	563-3305
Robert	1701 Octavia St	24	French	15-25	931-1030
Romano's	2030 Lombard St	7	Neapolitan	8-14	346-9193
Ronaynes	1799 Lombard St	11	Seafood	12-20	922-5060
Ruby's	500 Brannan St	65	American	10-19	495-0457
Russian Renaissance	5241 Geary Blvd	47	Russian	15-20	752-8558
Sagami-Ya	1525 Irving St	62	Chinese	6-9	661-2434
Sanpei	1581 Webster St	31	Japanese	6-10	922-2290
Sanppo	1702 Post St	25	Japanese	10-19	346-3486
Tai Ho	6253 Geary Blvd	44	Chinese	5-8	668-5811
Thanh Long	4101 Judah St	61	Vietnamese	8-13	665-1146
Tien Fu	1395 Noriega St	64	No Chinese	9-13	665-1064
Tora-Ya	1914 Fillmore St	21	Japanese	8-13	931-9455
Vegi-Food	1820 Clement St	40	Vegetarian	7-12	387-8111
Vlasta's Czechoslovak	2420 Lombard St	4	Hungarian	8-13	931-7533
Yet Wah	2140 Clement St	37	No Chinese	4-9	387-8040
Yoshida-ya	2909 Webster St	14	Japanese	12-20	346-3431

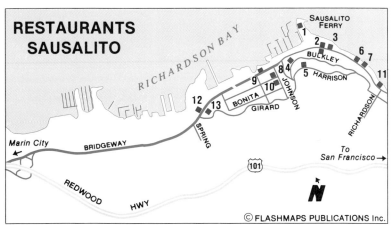

SAUSALITO RESTAURANTS

Restaurant	Address	Map No	Cuisine	Price ★	Telephone
Alta Mira	126 Harrison	5	Continental	8-15	332-1350
Casa Madrone	801 Bridgeway	4	Light French	12-18	332-1350
Cat 'n Fiddle	681 Bridgeway	2	American	5-8	332-4912
Chart House	201 Bridgeway	11	American	12-20	332-0804
Christophe's	1919 Bridgeway	13	French	14-22	332-9244
Flynn's Landing	303 Johnson St	10	Seafood	8-15	332-0131
Greater Gatsby	39 Caledonia St	8	Pizza	5-10	332-4500
Guernica	2009 Bridgeway	12	French	12-20	332-1512
Houlihan's Old Place	660 Bridgeway	3	American	10-15	332-8512
Horizon	558 Bridgeway	7	Continental	10-20	331-3232
Ondine	558 Bridgeway	7	Continental	20 +	332-0791
Scoma's	588 Bridgeway	6	Seafood	12-20	332-9551
Seven Seas	682 Bridgeway Ave	2	Seafood	8-20	332-1304
Spinnaker	100 Spinnaker Dr	1	Seafood	10-20	332-1500
Winship's	670 Bridgeway	3	American	5-9	332-1454
Zack's by the Bay	Bridgeway & Turney	9	American	4-8	332-9779

★ *Prices do not include drinks or gratuities.*

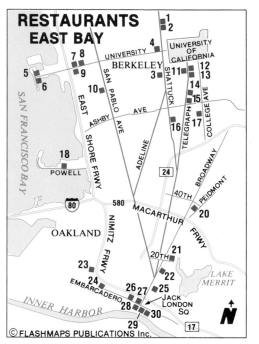

RESTAURANTS EAST BAY

1 Chez Panisse
2 Warszawa
3 Giovanni's
4 Taiwan
5 Solomon Grundy's
6 Hs Lordships
7 Spenger's Fish
8 Fourth St Grill
9 China Station
10 Nadine
11 Rainbow's End
12 Larry Blake's
13 Blue Nile
14 Casa de Eva
15 Augusta's
16 Metropole
16 Omnivore
17 Norman's
18 Trader Vic's
20 Bay Wolf
21 Mirabeau
22 Chez Lucien
23 Love's Pagan Den
24 Roaring Camp Cafe
25 Silver Dragon
26 Rusty Scupper
27 Capri
28 Gallagher's
29 El Caballo
30 Lorenzo's

© FLASHMAPS PUBLICATIONS Inc.

EAST BAY RESTAURANTS—ALPHABETICAL

Restaurant	Address	Map No.	Cuisine	Average Price ★	Telephone
Augusta's	2955 Telegraph Ave	15	Seafd/Ital	$10-20	548-3140
Bay Wolf Cafe	3853 Piedmont Ave	20	French	10-20	655-6004
Blue Nile	2525 Telegraph Ave	13	Ethiopian	7-12	540-6777
Capri	1103 Embarcadero	27	Ital Sfd	9-16	839-4800
Casa de Eva	2826 Telegraph Ave	14	Mexican	5-9	540-9092
Chez Lucien	1739 Broadway	22	French	15-25	834-7363
Chez Panisse	1517 Shattuck	1	Continental	20-25	548-5525
China Station	700 University	9	Cantonese	5-9	548-7880
El Caballo	70 Jack London Sq	29	Mexican	10-17	835-9260
Fourth Street Grill	1820 4th St	8	Italian	8-12	849-0526
Gallagher's	86 Jack London Sq	28	Steak/Sfd	8-14	893-5292
Giovanni's	2420 Shattuck	3	Italian	9-14	843-6678
Hs Lordships	199 Seawall Dr	6	Amer/Cont	10-20	843-2733
Larry Blake's	2367 Telegraph Ave	12	Fr/Cont	9-14	848-0886
Lorenzo's	55 Alice, Jack London	30	Italian	9-15	465-4876
Love's Pagan Den	760 East 8th St	23	Polynesian	6-15	832-3383
Metropole	2271 Shattuck Ave	16	French	20-25	848-3080
Mirabeau	Kaiser Center	21	Fr/Cont	20-30	834-6575
Nadine	2400 San Pablo	10	Continental	10-20	549-2807
Normans	3204 College Ave	17	Continental	8-14	655-5291
Omnivore	3015 Shattuck	16	French	10-15	848-4346
Rainbow's End	2428 Telegraph Ave	11	Korean	4-7	843-7739
Roaring Camp Cafe	571 Fifth St	24	International	8-15	451-0863
Rusty Scupper	15 Embarcadero W	26	Stks/Sfd	10-20	465-0105
Silver Dragon	835 Webster	25	Chinese	8-15	893-3748
Solomon Grundys	100 Seawall Dr	5	Seafood	9-16	548-1876
Spengers Fish	1919 4th St	7	Seafood	5-10	845-7771
Taiwan	2071 University Ave	4	Chinese	5-10	845-1456
Trader Vic's	9 Anchor Dr	18	Polynesian	14-25	653-3400
Warszawa	1730 Shattuck Ave	2	Polish	10-15	841-5539

★ Prices do not include drinks or gratuities

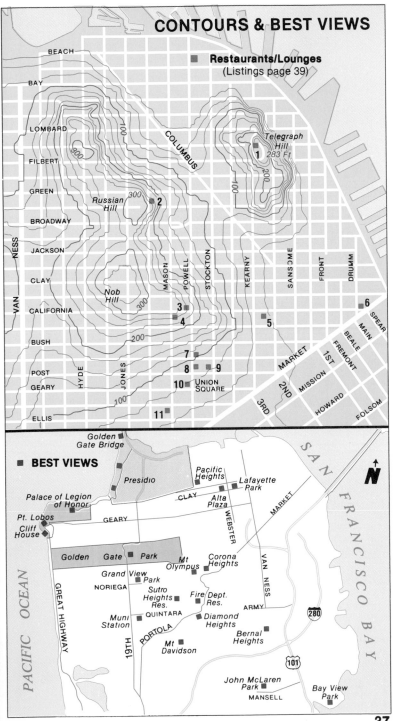

CONTOURS & BEST VIEWS

■ **Restaurants/Lounges**
(Listings page 39)

Telegraph Hill
283 Ft
1

COLUMBUS

BEACH
BAY
LOMBARD
FILBERT
GREEN
BROADWAY
JACKSON
CLAY
CALIFORNIA
BUSH
POST
GEARY
ELLIS

VAN NESS

Russian Hill
2

Nob Hill

HYDE
JONES
MASON
POWELL
STOCKTON
KEARNY
SANSOME
FRONT
DRUMM
SPEAR
MAIN
BEALE
FREMONT
1ST
2ND
3RD

6
5
3
4
7
8
9
10 UNION SQUARE
11

MARKET
MISSION
HOWARD
FOLSOM

■ **BEST VIEWS**

Golden Gate Bridge

Presidio

Pacific Heights
Lafayette Park

Palace of Legion of Honor

Pt. Lobos
Cliff House

CLAY
Alta Plaza
WEBSTER

GEARY

Golden Gate Park

Mt Olympus

Corona Heights

VAN NESS

MARKET

PACIFIC OCEAN

GREAT HIGHWAY

Grand View Park

NORIEGA

Sutro Heights Res.

Fire Dept. Res.

Muni Station

QUINTARA

PORTOLA

19TH

Mt Davidson

Diamond Heights

Bernal Heights

ARMY

280

John McLaren Park

MANSELL

Bay View Park

101

SAN FRANCISCO BAY

N

37

NIGHT LIFE—BY MAP NUMBER

NIGHT LIFE—ALPHABETICAL

Place	Address	Map No	Type	Telephone
Alexis Cellar/Disco	1001 California	21	Piano/Disco	771-1001
Bajones	1062 Valencia St	off map	Blues/Jazz	282-2522
Barnaby's	1 Embarcadero Ctr	23	Live Rock/Dancing	956-8768
Caesar's Palace	3140 Mission St	off map	Salsa Band/Dancing	826-1179
Casablanca	2323 Polk St	3	Piano entertainment	441-2244
Chi Chi Club	440 Broadway	14	Revue Comedy*	392-6213
Club Fugazi	678 Green St	7	Comedy/music revu*	421-4222
Condor Nightclub	300 Columbus Ave	10	Topless Carol Doda	392-4443
Earthquake McGn	Pier 39	24	Dixieland	986-1433
Finocchio's	506 Broadway	9	Comedy/Imperson*	982-9388
Ghiradelli Cellar	900 Northpoint St	1	Folk Music	776-5021
Great Amer Music	859 O'Farrell St	32	Pop/Jazz headlners*	885-0750
Greek Taverna	256 Columbus Ave	12	Greek music/dancing	362-7260
Hyatt Rgncy Atrium	5 Embarcadero Ctr	25	Dancing big band	788-1234
I. Beam	1748 Haight St	off map	80's rock disco(gay)*	668-6006
Kabuki Nightclub	1881 Post St	off map	Jazz/rock, comedy*	362-0261
Kimball's	300 Grove St	off map	Music, revues*	861-5585
La Pinata	510 Larkin Ave	33	Live entertainment	771-1850
Last Day Saloon	406 Clement St	off map	Live Band	387 6343
Lord Jim's	1500 Broadway	4	Piano/Entertainment	928-3015
Mr. Hydes	1390 California St	19	Jazz/Pop	775-7574
Music Hall Theatre	931 Larkin St	31	Dance revue*	776-8996
New Orleans Rm	Fairmont Hotel	20	Pop/Jazz headliners	772-5259
1906 Lounge	Holiday Inn	18	Disco/Dancing	441-4000
Old Spaghetti	478 Green St	8	Comedy/Impro	776-2511
On Broadway	435 Broadway	17	Revues*	398-0800
Other Cafe, The	100 Carl St	off map	Comedy	681-0748
Oz Room	St Francis Hotel	30	Pop/reggae/jazz	397-7000
Palladium, The	1031 Kearny St	16	Disco dancing*	434-1308
Plush Room	940 Sutter St	27	Pop/Jazz revues	885-6800
Punch Line	444 A Battery St	22	Comedy*	474-3801
Reflections-Hyatt	345 Stockton St	29	Pop/Niteclub	398-1234
Regent Cafe	950 Clement St	off map	Band/disco dancing	752-0354
Savoy Tivoli	1434 Grant Ave	5	Revues/Music*	362-7023
Starlite Room	Sir Francis Drake	28	Dancing	392-7755
Stone, The	412 Broadway	15	Rock*	391-8282
Trocadero-Transfer	520 4th Street	off map	Discotheque*	495-6620
Washington Sq Bar	1707 Powell St	6	Jazz piano	982-8123
Wolfgang's	901 Columbus Ave	2	Rock video, Reggae*	441-4333

*COVER OR ADMISSION

RESTAURANTS & LOUNGES WITH BEST VIEWS
Located on Map Page 37

Place	Location	Map No	Comment
Carnelian Room	555 California St	5	Cocktails-52nd floor Bank Amer
Coit Tower	Telegraph Hill	1	Available for private parties
Coolbreth Park	Taylor & Broadway	2	Bring your own picnic
Fairmont Hotel	950 Mason St	3	Cocktails-Crown Rm 29th fl
Holiday -Union Sq	480 Sutter St	7	Cocktails-Public House 30th floor
Hyatt Regency	5 Embarcadero Ctr	6	Equinox Dining rm-18th floor
Hyatt-Union Sq	345 Stockton St	9	Hugo's Dining rm -36th floor
Mark Hopkins	California & Mason	4	Cocktails-Top of the Mark-19th floor
St Francis Hotel	Union Square	10	Cocktails-Oz Room-32nd floor
SF Hilton	Mason & O'Farrell	11	Henri's Dining rm -46th floor
Sir Francis Drake	Sutter & Powell Sts	8	Cocktails-Starlite Roof-21st floor

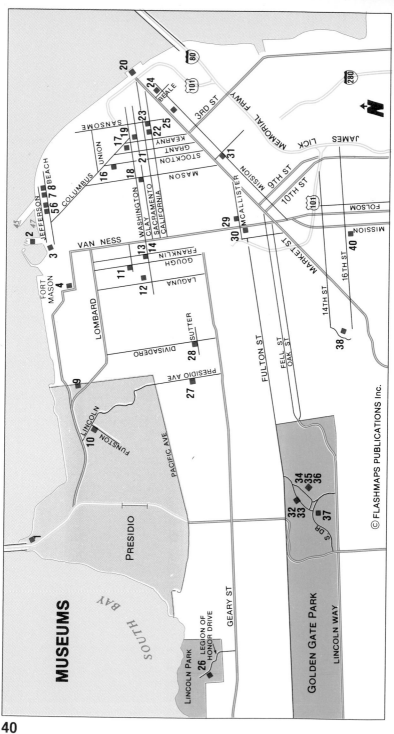

MUSEUMS

SOUTH BAY

PRESIDIO

Lincoln Park

LEGION OF HONOR DRIVE

26

GEARY ST

GOLDEN GATE PARK

LINCOLN WAY

Fort Mason

VAN NESS

JEFFERSON

BEACH

Columbus

Union

SANSOME

Washington

Clay

Sacramento

California

KEARNY

GRANT

STOCKTON

MASON

FRANKLIN

GOUGH

LAGUNA

LOMBARD

DIVISADERO

SUTTER

PRESIDIO AVE

PACIFIC AVE

LINCOLN

FUNSTON

BEALE

3RD ST

MEMORIAL FRWY

LICK

JAMES

9TH ST

MISSION

McALLISTER

10TH ST

FULTON ST

FELL ST

OAK ST

MARKET ST

14TH ST

16TH ST

FOLSOM

MISSION

© FLASHMAPS PUBLICATIONS Inc.

40

MUSEUMS—BY MAP NUMBERS

1 Fort Point	8 Wax Museum	18 Chinese	31 Old Mint
2 SF Maritime	9 Exploratorium	22 Wells Fargo	32 De Young
3 SF Maritime Pk	10 Presidio Army	23 Money of Amer	33 Asian Art
4 Italo-Americano	11 Octagon House	24 Energy Expo	34 CA. Aca Sci
4 Liberty Ship	12 CA. Historical	25 Chevron Oil	35 Morrison P.
4 Mexican	13 Haas-Lilienthal	26 CA. Palace Leg	36 Steinhart Aquar
4 SF Afri-Amer	14 SF Architect.	27 Pioneer Mem	37 Strybing Arbor
5 Wharf Wax	16 North Beach	28 Russian	38 Randall Jr
6 Guinness	17 Chinese Hist	29 Soc CA. Pioneer	40 Missn Dolores
7 Ripley's	18 Cable Car	30 SF Modern Art	

MUSEUMS—ALPHABETICAL

Museum	Address	Map No.	Telephone
Asian Art (Avery Brundage)	Golden Gate Park	33	558-2993
Cable Car Barn	Washington & Mason	18	474-1887
California Academy Sciences	Golden Gate Park	34	221-5100
California Historical Society	2090 Jackson St	12	567-1848
California Palace of Legion Honor	Lincoln Park	26	221-4811
Chevron Oil Museum	555 Market Street	25	894-7700
Chinese Cultural Found	750 Kearny St - 3rd Fl	19	986-1822
Chinese Historical Society	17 Adler Place	17	391-1188
De Young, M.H. Memorial	Golden Gate Park	32	221-8394
Energy Expo(Pacifc Gas&Elec)	77 Beale St	24	781-4211
Exploratorium-Palace Fine Arts	3601 Lyon Street	9	563-7337
Fort Point National Historic	Presidio	1	556-2857
Guinness World Records	235 Jefferson St	6	771-9890
Haas-Lilienthal House	2007 Franklin St	13	441-3004
Italo-Americano Museum	Fort Mason, Bldg C	4	673-2200
Liberty Ship - SS Jeremiah O'Brien	Fort Mason, Pier 3	4	441-3101
Mexican Museum	Fort Mason, Bldg.D	4	441-0404
Mission Dolores	Dolores & 16th St	40	621-8203
Money of American West	Bank Calif. 400 Calif St	23	765-2189
Morrison Planetarium	Golden Gate Park	35	752-8268
North Beach Museum	1435 Stockton St	16	626-7070
Oakland Museum	1000 Oak St, Oakland	off map	273-3401
Octagon House-Col. Dames	2645 Gough St	11	885-9796
Old Mint	Fifth & Mission Sts	31	974-0788
Pioneer Memorial	655 Presidio Ave	27	861-8000
Presidio Army Museum	Lincoln Blvd & Funston	10	561-4115
Randall, Josephine Jr. Museum	199 Museum Way	38	863-1399
Ripley's Believe or Not	175 Jefferson St	7	771-6188
Russian Culture Museum	2450 Sutter St.	28	929-9741
S. F. African-American Historic	Fort Mason, Bldg. C	4	441-0640
S. F. Architect. Heritage	2007 Franklin St	14	441-3000
San Francisco Maritime Museum	Aquatic Park on Polk	3	673-0797
San Francisco Maritime Historic	Hyde & Beach St	2	556-2904
San Francisco Mus Modern Art	McAllister St Van Ness	30	863-8800
Society of California Pioneers	456 McAllister St	29	861-5278
Steinhart Aquarium Calif Aca Sci	Golden Gate Park	36	221-4214
Strybing Arboretum	So Dr. Golden Gate Pk	37	661-1316
Wax Mus-Fisherman's Wharf	145 Jefferson St	8	885-4834
Wells Fargo	464 California St	22	396-2619
Wharf Wax Life	295 Jefferson St	5	885-5656

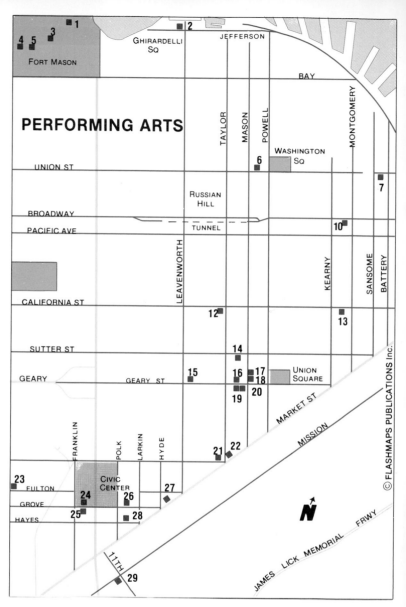

PERFORMING ARTS

PERFORMING ARTS—ALPHABETICAL

Theater	Address	Map No.	Telephone
Alcazar	650 Geary Street	15	775-7100
American Conservatory	450 Geary Street	16	673-6440
Asian American	Fort Mason Bldg B	5	928-8922
Brooks Hall	Civic Center	26	974-4000
Cannery Theater	2801 Leavenworth	2	441-6800
Centerspace	2840 Mariposa St	★	861-5059
Civic Auditorium	Civic Center	28	974-4000
Cole Hall	500 Parnassus (UCSF)	★	666-2019
Curran Theater	445 Geary Street	19	673-4400
Davies Symphony Hall	Van Ness & Grove	25	431-5400
Fort Mason People's Coalition	Buchanan & Marina	4	776-8999
Geary Theater	415 Geary Street	20	673-6440
Giannini Auditorium	555 California St	13	622-2080
Golden Gate	Taylor & Market	21	775-8800
Herbst Theater	Civic Center	24	392-4400
Icehouse	151 Union St	7	421-6300
Intersection	756 Union St	6	982-2356
Little Theater	Palace Legion Honor	★	221-4811
Magic Theater	Bldg D, Fort Mason	3	441-8001
Marine's Memorial	609 Sutter St	14	673-6672
Masonic Auditorium	1111 California St	12	776-4917
McKenna Auditorium	SF State University	★	469-2411
Music Hall	931 Larkin St	★	824-8844
On Broadway	435 Broadway	10	398-0800
One Act Theater	430 Mason Street	18	421-6162
Orpheum	Market & Hyde Streets	27	474-3800
Performing Arts Center	Van Ness & Hayes	25	621-6600
Presentation	2350 Turk Blvd	★	752-7755
SF Ballet	455 Franklin at Fulton	24	861-5600
SF Conserv Music	1201 Ortega St	★	564-8086
SF Moving Company	186 Clara	29	495-5844
SF School of Drama	Bldg C Fort Mason	1	885-2766
Sigmund Stern Mem Grove	19th & Sloat Blvd	★	558-4728
Theatre on Square	450 Post St	17	433-9500
Victoria	2961 16th St	★	863-7576
Warfield Theater	982 Market St	22	775-7722
War Memorial Opera House	Van Ness & Grove St	24	864-3330
Western Addition Cultural	762 Fulton St	23	921-7976

PERFORMING ARTS — BAY AREA

Berkeley Repertory	2025 Addison St, Berkeley	845-4700
Concord Pavilion	2000 Kirker Pass Rd, Concord	676-8742
Dinkelspiel Aud	Stanford University, Palo Alto	366-9561
Hertz Hall	U of California, Berkeley	642-2698
Julia Morgan Center	2640 College Ave, Berkeley	548-7234
Kaiser Convention Ctr	10 Tenth St, Oakland	839-7500
Marin Co Civic Ctr	Civic Center, San Rafael	472-3500
Oakland Civic Theater	666 Belleveue Ave, Oakland	452-2909
Oakland Coliseum	Hegenberger/Nimitz Frwy, Oakland	639-7700
Paramount Theater	2025 Broadway, Oakland	893-2300
San Mateo Perform Arts	600 N Delaware, San Mateo	348-8243
Trinity Center	2320 Dana St, Berkeley	549-3864
Woodminster Amphitheater	3300 Joaquin Miller Rd, Oakland	531-9597
Zellerbach Auditorium	U of California, Berkeley	642-9988

★ off map

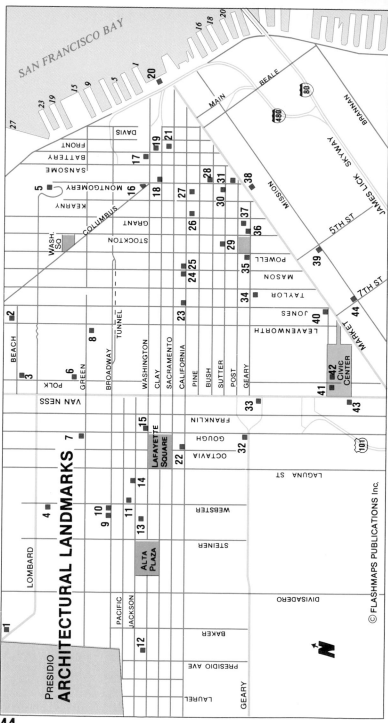

ARCHITECTURAL LANDMARKS

PRESIDIO

SAN FRANCISCO BAY

© FLASHMAPS PUBLICATIONS Inc.

LAFAYETTE SQUARE

ALTA PLAZA

WASH. SQ.

CIVIC CENTER

ARCHITECTURE & HISTORIC LANDMARKS

Building	Architect	Map No.	Date
Alcoa Building	Skidmore Owings & Merrill	19	1964
Alhambra Theater	Miller & Pflueger	6	1926
Atherton House (Rathbone)	Unknown	22	1883
Bank of America World Hdq	Wurster Bernardi-Skidmore Owng	27	1970-71
Bourne Mansion	Willis Polk	11	1894
Calif Hist Soc (Whittier Hse)	E.R.Swain & N.J. Tharp	14	1894-96
Calvary Presbyterian	Unknown	13	1901
Cannery	Joseph Esherick & Associates	2	c1909
Casebolt House	Unknown	pg. 46	1865-66
Chrysler Showroom	Bernard Maybeck	33	1928
City Hall (Civic Center)	Bakewell & Brown	42	1915
City of Paris Liberty House	Clinton Day	36	1900
Coit Tower	Arthur Brown Jr	5	1934
Conservatory	Lord & Burnham	pg. 51	1875
Davies, Louise K Symphony	Skidmore Owings & Merrill	43	1981
De Young Museum	Louis Christian Mullgardt	pg. 61	1916
Embarcadero Center	John Portman & Associates	21	1971
Fairmont Hotel	Reid Brothers	25	1906
Ferry Building	A. Page Brown	20	1896
Feusier Octagon House	Unknown	8	1857
Flood Mansion (Pac Union)	Augustus Laver & Willis Polk	24	1885-86
Flood Mansion (Convent)	Bliss & Faville	9	1916
Garden Court Palace Hotel	Trowbridge & Livingston	38	1909
Geary Theater	Bliss & Faville	34	1910
Ghirardelli Square	William Mooser	3	c1860
Golden Gate Bridge	Irving Morrow-Joseph Strauss	pg. 5	1927
Grace Cathedral	Lewis P. Hobart	23	1928
Grant House	Hiss & Weekes	10	1910
Haas-Lilienthal House	Unknown	pg. 46	1886
Hallidie Building	Willis Polk & Co.	30	1917
Helga Howie Boutique	Frank Lloyd Wright	37	1949
Hibernian Bank	Albert Pissis	40	1892
Holy Virgin Russn Orth Cath	Unknown	off map	1880
Japanese Tea House	George Turner Marsh	pg. 51	1893-94
Medical-Dental Office Bldg	Timothy Pflueger	29	1930
Mills Bldg & Tower	Burnham & Root	28	1892
Mission Dolores St. Francis	Willis Polk (restored 1918)	off map	1782
Octagon House	Orson Fowler	7	1857
Old Fugazi Bldg Bank Italy	Field & Kohlberg	16	1911
Old Mint	A. B. Mullett	39	1869-74
Old St. Mary's Church	Craine-England (restored 1969)	26	1853-54
Palace of Fine Arts	Bernard Maybeck	1	1915
Palace of Legion of Honor	George A. Applegarth	pg. 40	1916
Phelps, Abner House	Unknown	off map	c1850
Spreckels Mansion	George Applegarth	15	1913
St. Francis Hotel	Bliss & Faville	35	1904-08
St. Mary's Cathedral	Belluschi Nervi McSweeney Ryan	32	1971
Swedenborgian	A. Page Brown	12	1894
Transamerica Pyramid	William Pereira & Assoc	18	1972
U. S. Customhouse	Eames & Young	17	1906-11
US Post Office & Fed Court	James Knox Taylor	44	1905
Vendanta Society Hdqtrs	Joseph A. Leonard	4	1905
War Mem Opera House	Brown & Lands	41	1932
Wells Fargo Building	John Graham & Co.	31	1966

SEE PAGE 46 FOR VICTORIAN HOUSES

Map labels (streets): FILBERT, UNION, GREEN, VALLEJO, BROADWAY, PACIFIC, JACKSON, WASHINGTON, CLAY, SACRAMENTO, CALIFORNIA, PINE, BUSH, SUTTER, POST, GEARY, O'FARRELL, ELLIS

OCTAVIA, GOUGH, FILMORE, WEBSTER, BUCHANNAN, FRANKLIN, VAN NESS, LAGUNA, STEINER, PIERCE, SCOTT, DIVISADERO, BRODERICK, BAKER

VICTORIAN HOUSES

ALTA PLAZA

LAFAYETTE PARK

© FLASHMAPS PUBLICATIONS Inc.

VICTORIAN HOUSES—BY MAP NUMBER

Name or Site	Year	Map No.	Style and Interesting Feature
2460 Union Street	c1872	1	Victorian Gothic · Mansard roof
James Cudworth House	1874	2	Italianate with bay windows
1980 Union Street	c1870	3	3 Victorian buildings now housing shops
St.MaryVirginEpiscopal	1891	4	Victorian Gothic
Sherman House	1879	5	Victorian Baroque
1950-58-60 Green Street	c1875	6	Italianate flat front
Casebolt House*	1865/66	7	Italian villa
1772 Vallejo Street	1875	8	Italianate, architect: Edmund Wharff
Leale House	c1850	9	Italianate facade farm house
2000 Pacific Avenue	1894	10	Queen Anne tower, stained glass
Talbot-Dutton House*	1869	11	Italianate slanted bay windows
3022 Washington Street	1893	12	SF Stick, architects:Henricksen-Mahoney
2773-81-87 Clay Street	1890	13	SF Stick with fancywork,millwork,art glss
2637 to 2673 Clay St	c1870	14	11 Italianate bay & flat front windows
2209 to 2253 Webster St	1878	15	Italianate slanted bays-5 & 3 house group
Haas-Lilienthal House*	1886	16	Queen Anne tower-Baroque-Italianate
1805 · 1807 Baker St	1882	17	Cottages with Mansard roofs
Ortman-Shumate*	1870	18	Italianate with bay windows
1990 California Street*	1882	19	SF Stick-Eastlake-Queen Anne
1976 California Street	1883	20	Italianate SF Stick, Arch:Schmidt-Havens
1834 California Street*	1876	21	Queen Anne tower-fine details
Lilienthal-Orville Pratt*	1876	22	Italianate with bay windows
1701 Franklin Street*	1895	23	Queen Anne tower
1737 Webster Street	1885	24	SF Stick with ornate details
1717 Webster Street	1875	25	Italiante with flat front
2006 · 2076 Bush St	1852-78	26	2006 *Italianate bay windows
1801 · 1865 Laguna St	1889	27	SF Stick-11 houses by Wm Hinkel
1484 Post Street	1874	28	Italianate flat front
Beidman Place	c1875	29	Rehab Proj of Found SF Arch & SF Redev.

*Official San Francisco Landmark

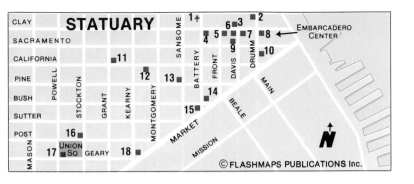

STATUES DOWNTOWN

SAN FRANCISCO TREASURES

Museums page 41

PARKS & RECREATION

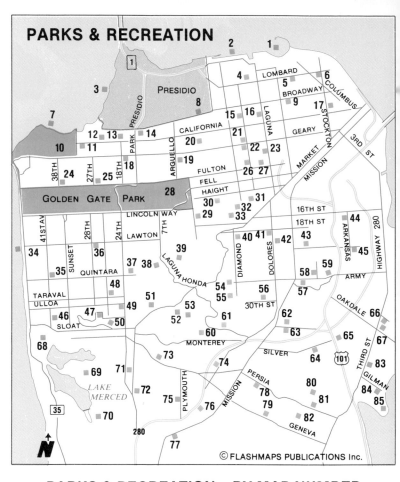

PARKS & RECREATION—BY MAP NUMBER

PARKS & RECREATION—BY MAP NUMBER (Continued)

57 Bernal Heights	67 Joseph Lee	76 Cayuga
58 Garfield Square	68 Fleishacker Zoo	77 Alice Chalmers
59 Rolph	69 Harding	78 Excelsior
60 Sunnyside	69 Fleming	79 Crocker-Amazon
61 Glen Park	70 Lake Merced	80 Louis Sutter
62 Holly Park	71 Junipero Serra	81 McLaren Park
63 St. Mary's	72 Merced Heights	82 Francis J. Herz
64 Portola	73 Aptos	83 Bay View
65 Silver Terrace	74 Balboa Park	84 Gilman
66 Galvez	75 Ocean View	85 Bay View

PARKS & RECREATION—ALPHABETICAL

Park & (acres)	Address	Map No	Sports Facilities
Alamo Square (12.7)	Hayes & Steiner	26	1 tennis court, bay view
Alice Chalmers (1.7)	Brunswick & Whittier	77	1 tennis court, playground
Alice Marble (2.6)	Greenwich & Hyde	5	3 tennis courts
Alta Plaza (11.9)	Jackson & Steiner	15	3 tennis courts
Aptos (4.6)	Aptos & Ocean Ave	73	softball, playground, 1 tennis
Argonne (.83)	18th Ave & Geary	18	1 tennis court, playground
Aquatic Park (35)	Beach & Polk St	1	swimming, walking, fishing
Bakers Beach	Presidio & Lincoln Blvd	3	swimming, walking, fishing
Balboa Park (27.5)	Ocean & San Jose	74	softball, baseball, tennis, soccer
Bay View (26.1)	Le Conte Ave	85	no sports facilities
Bay View (3.4)	3rd & Armstrong	83	baseball, ML King pool (822-5707)
Bernal Heights (20.2)	Bernal Heights Blvd	57	no sports facilities
Buena Vista (36.0)	Buena Vista & Haight	30	2 tennis courts
Cabrillo (.83)	38th Ave & Cabrillo	24	1 tennis, playground
Cayuga (2.9)	Cayuga & Naglee	76	1 tennis, playground
Chinese (.65)	Sacramento & Wavrly	17	play apparatus, 1 tennis
Christopher (6.7)	Diamond Hts & Duncan	55	softball, playground, 1 tennis
Crocker-Amazon (54.9)	Geneva & Moscow	79	soft/baseball, soccer, 3 tennis
Douglass (7.2)	26th & Douglass	54	softball, play apparatus, tennis
Duboce Recreation (4.2)	Duboce & Scott	31	basketball
Dupont (.83)	30th Ave & Clement	11	4 tennis courts
Eureka Valley (1.9)	Collingwood/18th St	40	softball, basketball, tennis
Excelsior (1.6)	Russia & Madrid	78	softball, 1 tennis, play area
Fleishacker Zoo (136.4)	Sloat Blvd & 45th	68	children's playfield, picnicking
Fleming Golf Course	Lake Merced	69	9-hole golf (tel. 661-1865)
Folsom (.78)	Folsom & 21st	43	1 tennis, play apparatus
Fulton (.83)	Fulton & 27th Ave	25	1 tennis, playground
Funston Rec (12.5)	Chesnut & Buchanan	4	4 tennis, basketball
Galvez (6.2)	3rd St & Galvez	66	playfield, Coleman playground
Garfield Square (2.9)	Harrison & 25th St	58	pool (tel. 824-4949) playfield
Gilman (7.0)	Gilman & Griffith	84	softball, playground
Glen Pk Canyon (41.8)	Chenery & Elk	61	Silvr Tree camp, sft/bsebll tennis
Golden Gate (1017.4)	For details see pg 51	28	9-hole golf, soccer, 21 tennis
Grattan (1.5)	Stanyan & Alma	29	softball, playground
Hamilton Rec (3.97)	Geary & Steiner	21	pool (tel. 931-2450), 2 tennis
Harding Pk Golf	Lake Merced	69	18-hole golf (tel. 664-4690)
Harvey Milk Center	50 Scott St	31	dance & music (tel. 558-4277)
Hayes Valley (.6)	Hayes & Buchanan	27	1 tennis, playground
Hayward/Lang Field (5.3)	Turk & Octavia	23	softball, 2 tennis
Helen Wills (3.98)	Broadway & Larkin	9	1 tennis, playground
Herz (3.4)	University & Hahn	82	Coffman pool (586-8570), tennis
Holly Park (7.5)	Holly Circle Highland	62	1 tennis court
Jackson (4.4)	Carolina & 17th St	44	soft/baseball, 1 tennis

49

PARKS & RECREATION—ALPHABETICAL (Continued)

Park & (acres)	Address	Map No	Sports Facilities
Joseph Lee Rec (1.8)	Oakdale & Mendell	67	basketball, 1 tennis
J.P. Murphy (.49)	1960 Ninth Ave	38	playground, 3 tennis
Julius Kahn (7.3)	Pacific Ave & Spruce	8	softball, 4 tennis
Junipero Serra (1.5)	300 Stonecrest Dr	71	playground, 1 tennis
Kimbell (5.4)	Pierce & Ellis	22	softball, baseball,playground
Lafayette Sq (11.5)	Washington & Laguna	16	2 tennis, playfields
Lake Merced (700.5)	Skyline Blvd	70	boating fresh water fishing sailr
Larsen (6.6)	Wawona & 19th Ave	49	pool(tel.661-1475)softball tenn
Laurel Hill (1.4)	Euclid & Collins	20	softball, tennis, playground
Lincoln Park (204.06)	34th Ave & Clement	10	18-hole golf (tel.221-9911)
Louis Sutter (17.04)	University & Wayland	80	softball,2 tennis,playground
Marina Green (74.2)	Marina Blvd to Octavia	2	boating,fishing,walking,sailir
McCoppin Square (7.6)	Taraval & 24th Ave	48	softball,2 tennis, playground
McLaren Pk (317.8)	Visitacion Valley	81	amphitheater,softball,2 tenni
Merced Heights (1.03)	Bixbee & Shields	72	playground, 1 tennis
Midtown Terrace (13.4)	Clarendon & Olympia	39	4 tennis, playground
Miraloma (2.3)	Omar & Sequoia	53	softball, 1 tennis, playground
Mission (1.08)	Linda & 19th St	42	pool (tel.282-6950)2 tennis
Mission Dolores (13.4)	Dolores & 19th St	41	6 tennis courts
Moffet/Parkside(2.9)	26th & Vicente	47	softball, 4 tennis courts
Mountain Lake (15.0)	Lake & 12th Ave	14	4 tennis
Mt. Davidson (39.4)	Myra Way	52	climb 940' for 180° view
North Beach (2.5)	Mason & Lombard	6	pool(tel.421-7466)3 tennis plyg
Ocean Beach	48th & Pt Lobos	34	walkng,sunbathe no swimmr
Ocean View Rec (10.3)	Capital & Montana	75	soft/baseball,bsktbll,2 tennis
Phelan Beach	28th & Sea Cliff Ave	7	600' beach swimming, picnic
Portola Rec (4.95)	Felton & Holyoke	64	soft/baseball,basketball,tenr
Potrero Hill (9.5)	Arkansas & 22nd St	45	soft/baseball,basketball,tenr
Richmond (.83)	18th & Lake	13	1 tennis, playground
Rochambeau (.83)	24th Ave & Lake	12	1 tennis, playground
Rolph (3.08)	Potrero & Army	59	softball, 2 tennis
Rossi (6.5)	Arguello & Anza	19	softball,tennis,pool(751-9411
Sharp Park Golf	Pacifica on Hwy 1	off map	18-hole golf (tel.355-2862)
Sidney Peixotto (1.5)	15th & Roosevelt Way	32	2 tennis, playground
Silver Terrace (5.6)	Thornton & Bayshore	65	soft/baseball,1 tennis,plygrnc
South Sunset (3.6)	40th & Vicente	46	softball, 1 tennis,playground
St. Mary's Rec(13.5)	Murray & Justin	63	soft/baseball,3 tennis,basktb
States Street (2.5)	States near Castro	33	2 tennis, playground
Stern Grove (27.1)	Sloat & 19th Ave	50	Pine Lake day camp, 2 tennis
Sunnyside (1.07)	Melrose & Edna	60	1 tennis, playground
Sunset Heights (4.9)	Rockridge & 12th Ave	37	2 tennis courts
Sunset Rec (3.3)	Lawton & 28th Ave	36	softball,2 tennis,basketball
Upper Noe Rec (2.5)	Day & Sanchez	56	softball, 1 tennis,basketball
West Portal (1.89)	Ulloa St & Lenox Way	51	1 tennis, playground
West Sunset (16.8)	39th/41st & Ortega	35	soft/baseball,playgrnd,tennis

AMERICAN YOUTH HOSTELS — Golden Gate Council Tel. 771-4646

Hostel	Address	Approx miles SF	Telephone
Golden Gate	Bldg.941 Fort Barry, Sausalito 94965	8	331-2777
Montara Lighthouse	P.O.Box 737,Montara 94037	25	728-7177
Pigeon Pt Lighthse	Pigeon Pt-Hwy 1 Pescadero 94060	50	879-0633
Point Reyes	P.O.Box 247, Point Reyes Sta 94956	48	669-7414
San Francisco	Bldg.240 Fort Mason SF 94123	0	771-7277

GOLDEN GATE PARK

Park Headquarters (558-3706)
MCLAREN LODGE
Kezar Stadium (664-3200)
Fuchsia Garden
Children's Playground
(MINIATURE FARM, MERRY-GO-ROUND)
21 Tennis Courts (566-4800)
Conservatory (558-3973)
(CHANGING EXHIBITS OF FLOWERS & PLANTS)
Bowling Green
Recreational Field
J McLaren Statue & Dell
(20 ACRES - 500 SPECIES RHODODENDRUMS)

Academy of Science (221-5100)
Morrison Planetarium (221-5100)
Steinhart Aquarium (221-4214)

Shakespeare Garden
Hall of Flowers (558-3622)
Music Concourse
TEMPLE OF MUSIC (SHELL)

De Young Museum (221-4811)
Asian Art Museum (558-2993)
(AVERY BRUNDAGE COLLECTION)

Japanese Tea Garden
(PAGODA-WATERFALL-WALKS-CHERRY TREES)
Strybing Arboretum (558-3622)
(MEDICAL-ROCK-FRAGRANCE-DEMO GARDENS)
Boating (752-0347)
(ROWING, PADDLE & ELECTRIC MOTORS)
Baseball Diamond
Lindley Meadow

Park Stadium (558-3541)
POLO MATCHES AND HIGH SCHOOL EVENTS

Senior Center (558-4952)

Riding Academy (668-7360)

Buffalo Paddock
(GOATS, DEER & BISON)
Anglers' Lodge/Fly-casting pool
Bercut Equestrian field

Golf Course (9 holes)
GOLF CLUBHOUSE (751-8987)

Archery Field
Dutch Windmill
(QUEEN WILHELMINA TULIP GARDEN)
Beach Chalet

Murphy Windmill

Park covers 1017 acres.
PLANNED BY: **William H. Hall**
DEVELOPED BY: **John McLaren.**

Map labels:
STANYAN STREET, WALLER, KEZAH DR, ARGUELLO, 6TH AVE, 8TH AVE, 10TH AVE, DRIVE, MIDDLE, SOUTH DR, DR, 9TH, BLVD, ST, FULTON, PARK PRESIDIO DR, KENNEDY DRIVE, Stow Lake, 19TH, TRANSVERSE, 25TH, 25TH, DRIVE, MIDDLE, SOUTH DR, LINCOLN, 30TH, Spreckels Lake, 36TH AVE, SUNSET BLVD, Lakes, JFK DR, DRIVE, CHAIN LAKES, Chain of, KENNEDY DR, 47TH, GREAT HIGHWAY, SOUTH DR

N

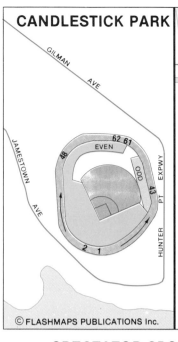

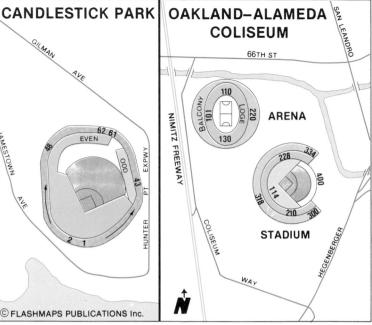

© FLASHMAPS PUBLICATIONS Inc.

SPECTATOR SPORTS—ALPHABETICAL

Sport	Playing Field	Address	Telephone
AUTO-RACING	Laguna Secca Rcwy	Monterey	*(408)* 373-1811
BASEBALL:			
Oakland A's	Oakland Coliseum	Hegenberger Rd	638-0500
SF Giants	Candlestick Park	Hunters Point Expwy	467-8000
BASKETBALL:			
GS Warriors	Oakland Coliseum	Hegenberger Rd	638-6000
BOXING:			
Golden Gloves	Cow Palace	Geneva Av, Daly City	469-6000
FOOTBALL:			
Oakland Invaders	Oakland Coliseum	Hegenberger Rd	638-7800
SF 49er's	Candlestick Park	Hunters Point Expwy	468-2249
Shrine E/W Game	Stanford Stadium	Palo Alto	497-1021
GOLF:			
Crosby Pro Am (AT&T)	Pebble Beach	Monterey	*(408)* 649-1533
Pro Am Tournament	Harding Park	Lake Merced	664-4690
HORSE RACING & SHOWS:			
Grand Nat'l Rodeo	Cow Palace	Geneva Av, Daly City	469-6065
Thoroughbred/Hrnss	Bay Meadows Rcwy	San Mateo	574-7223
Thoroughbred	Golden Gate	Albany	526-3020
SF MARATHON:	GG Park Conservtry	Army & Third Street	681-2322
SOCCER:			
SF Fog (Indoor)	Cow Palace	Geneva Av, Daly City	777-0555
SF Soccer League	Balboa Stadium	San Jose & Ocean Av	863-8892
TENNIS:			
Avon National	Oakland Coliseum	Hegenberger Rd	639-7700
Trans America Open	Cow Palace	Geneva Av, Daly City	334-4405
YACHTING:	Yacht Racing Assoc	San Francisco Bay	771-9500

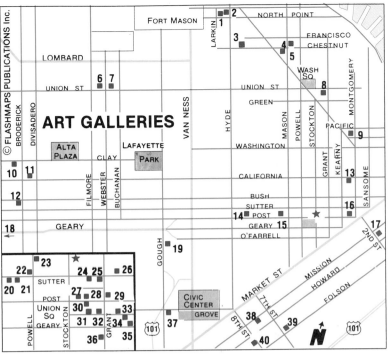

#	Gallery		#	Gallery		#	Gallery		#	Gallery
1	North Point		12	Jehu		23	Harcourt		31	Circle
2	Anneberg		13	Bank America		24	Wirtz		32	Conacher
3	SF Art Inst		14	Pence, John		25	Pascal		33	Thompson, Rich
4	Bonnafont		15	Stone, Will		26	Braunstein		34	Roberta English
5	Campbell		16	Stone, Jeremy		26	Quay		35	Anglim, Paule
6	Focus		17	Triangle		27	Reich		36	Fraenkel
7	Thackery & Robt		18	Bridge		27	Hunter		36	Ivory/Kimpton
8	Soker-Kaseman		19	Foster Goldstrom		28	Gump's		37	Vorpal
9	Montgomery		20	Iannetti, P		29	Fuller		38	Elliott
10	Sawyer, Wm		21	Maxwell		29	Berggruen		39	Source
11	Grapestake		22	Belcher, George		30	Allrich		40	Modernism

ART GALLERIES—ALPHABETICAL

Gallery	Address	Map No.	Gallery	Address	Map No.
Allrich	251 Post St	30	Ivory-Kimpton	55 Grant Ave	36
Anglim, Paule	14 Geary	35	Jehu	2719 Bush St	12
Anneberg	2719 Hyde St	2	Maxwell	551 Sutter St	21
Bank America	555 California	13	Montgomery	824 Montgomery	9
Belcher, Geo	500 Sutter St	22	Modernism	236 8th St	40
Berggruen	228 Grant Ave	29	North Point	872 North Point	1
Bonnafont	2200 Mason St	4	Pascal de Sarthe	315 Sutter St	25
Braunstein	254 Sutter St	26	Pence, John	750 Post St	14
Bridge	3010 Geary Blvd	18	Quay	254 Sutter St	26
Campbell, Chas.	647 Chestnut St	5	Reich, Dana	278 Post St	27
Circle	140 Maiden Lane	31	Roberta English	77 Maiden Lane	34
Conacher	134 Maiden Lane	32	SF Art Institute	800 Chestnut	3
Elliott, Doug	1151 Mission St	38	Sawyer, Wm	3045 Clay St	10
Focus	2146 Union St	6	Soker-Kasmn	1457 Grant Ave	8
Foster Goldst	1010 Gough St	19	Source	1099 Folsom St	39
Fraenkel	55 Grant Ave	36	Stone, Jeremy	126 Post St	16
Fuller/Goldeen	228 Grant Ave	29	Stone, Will	619 Post St	15
Grapestake	2876 California	11	Thackrey/Rbtson	2266 Union St	7
Gump's	250 Post St	28	Thompson, Rich.	80 Maiden Lane	33
Harcourt Cont	550 Powell	23	Triangle	95 Minna St	17
Hunter	278 Post St	27	Vorpal	393 Grove St	37
Iannetti, Pasq.	575 Sutter St	20	Wirtz, Stephen	345 Sutter St	24

53

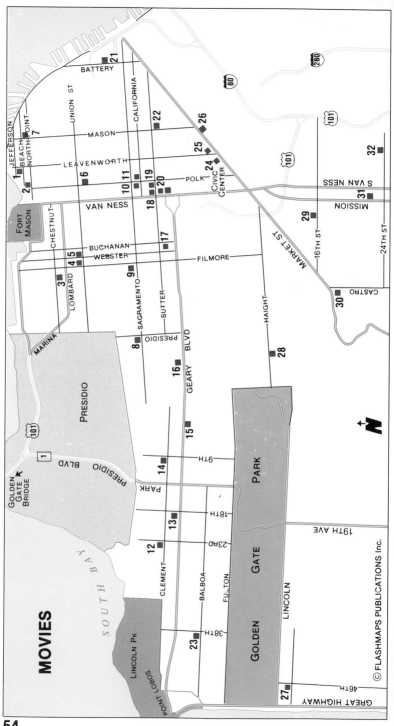

MOVIES

SAN FRANCISCO MOVIES—BY MAP NUMBER

1 Cannery	12 4 Star	23 Balboa
2 Ghirardelli Square	13 Alexandria	24 Embassy
3 Cinema 21	14 Coliseum	25 Strand
4 Metro II	15 Coronet	26 St. Francis 1 & 2
5 Metro Union	16 Bridge	27 Surf
6 Alhambra 1 & 2	17 Kokusai	28 Red Victorian
7 Northpoint	18 Regency 1	29 Roxie
8 Vogue	19 Regency 2	30 Castro
9 Clay	20 Centro Cedar	31 Grand
10 Royal-Polk	21 Gateway	32 York
11 Lumiere	22 SF Experience	

SAN FRANCISCO MOVIES—ALPHABETICAL

Theater	Address	Map No.	Telephone
Alexandria	5400 Geary Blvd	13	752-5100
Alhambra 1 & 2	Polk & Green	6	775-5656
Balboa	38th & Balboa	23	221-8181
Bridge	3010 Geary St	16	751-3212
Cannery Cinema	2801 Leavenworth	1	441-6800
Castro	429 Castro	30	621-6120
Cento Cedar	38 Cedar	20	776-8300
Cinema 21	2141 Chestnut	3	921-1234
Clay	2261 Fillmore	9	346-1123
Coliseum	Clement and 9th Ave	14	221-8181
Coronet	3575 Geary	15	752-4400
Embassy	1125 Market	24	431-5221
4 Star	2200 Clement	12	752-2650
Gateway	215 Jackson	21	421-3353
Ghirardelli Square	Beach & Polk Streets	2	441-7088
Grand	2665 Mission	31	648-3535
Kokusai	1700 Post	17	563-1400
Lumiere	1572 California	11	885-3200
Metro I	Union & Webster	5	221-8181
Metro II	2240 Union	4	221-8181
Northpoint	2290 Powell St	7	989-6060
Red Victorian	1659 Haight	28	863-3994
Regency 1	1320 Van Ness Ave	18	673-7141
Regency 2	1268 Sutter St	19	776-5505
Roxie	3117 16th St	29	863-1087
Royal	1529 Polk St	10	474-2131
SF Experience	420 Mason St	22	986-4767
St. Francis 1& 2	965 Market	26	362-4822
Strand	1127 Market	25	552-5990
Surf	Irving & 46th Ave	27	664-6300
Vogue	Sacramento & Presidio	8	221-8181
York	2789 24th St	32	282-0316

MOVIES Off Map

Empire	85 West Portal St	661-5110
Geneva (Drive-In)	Next to Cow Palace	587-2884
Plaza 1 & 2	311 Serramonte Plaza	756-3240
Spruce 4 (Drive-In)	South San Francisco	589-7965
Sea Vue Twin	Palmetto & W Manor Dr	359-5282
Serra	2710 Junipero Serra	755-1455
Serramonte 1, 2, 3, 4, 5, 6	4915 Junipero Serra	756-6500
Stonestown Twin	501 Buckingham Way	221-8181
Tanforan Park UA IV	El Camino Real & Sneath	588-0291

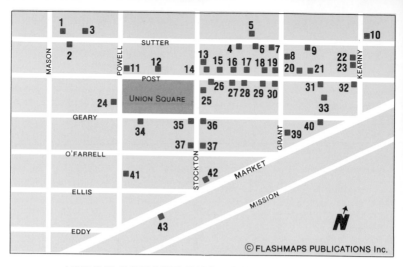

UNION SQUARE SHOPS & BOUTIQUES

1 Wm Sonoma
2 Jeffrey Davies
3 Forgotten
4 Jessica McClk
5 Wilkes Bshfrd
6 Louis Vuitton
7 Orpheus
8 Tiffany & Co
9 Firuze
10 B Dalton
11 Saks Fifth

12 Burberry
13 Wedgewood
14 Alfred Dunhill
15 Jaeger
16 Gumps
17 Eliz Arden
18 Eddie Bauer
19 Shreve's
20 Tom Wing
20 FAO Schwarz
21 Mark Cross

22 Helga Howie
23 Brass Boot
24 Maison Men
25 Bally Switz
26 Herbert's
27 Gucci
28 Barra Italy
29 Christian
30 Brooks Bros
31 Celine
32 Hastings

33 Covetry
34 Frank More
35 I Magnin
35 Laykin et Cie
36 Neiman Marcus
37 Macy's SF
39 My Child's
40 Lane Bryant
41 Books Inc
42 Grodin's
43 Emporium

SHOPS & BOUTIQUES — ALPHABETICAL

Shops	Address	Map No	Description	Telephone
Alfred Dunhill	290 Post	14	apparel, gifts, smoking access	781-3368
B. Dalton	200 Kearney	10	paperbacks and hard cover	956-2850
Bally of Switz	230 Stockton	25	quality shoes, leather goods	398-7463
Barra of Italy	245 Post	28	women's Italian knits & access	392-6452
Books Inc.	140 Powell	41	complete bookstore since 1851	397-1555
Brass Boot	125 Kearney	23	Handcrafted Italian footwear	397-5933
Brooks Brothers	201 Post	30	classic men & women clothes	397-4500
Burberry/Bullock	340 Post	12	Classic clothes & raingear	392-4243
Celine	155 Post	31	French boutique	397-1140
Christian of Copen	225 Post	29	household imports	392-3394
Covetry, The	50 Maiden Ln	33	custom design imported fabrics	986-8451
Eddie Bauer	220 Post	18	sports' Heaven	986-7600
Elizabeth Arden	230 Post	17	beauty services, womns access	982-3755
Emporium-Capwell	835 Market	43	complete department store	764-2222
F. A. O. Schwarz	180 Post	20	toy heaven - all ages	391-0100
Firuze	285 Sutter St	9	women's European designs, silks	986-1777
Forgotten Woman	550 Sutter	3	Fine designer classics 14-46	788-1452
Frank More	285 Geary	34	quality shoes & handbags	421-0356
Grodin's	798 Market	42	elegant men & women's wear	391-8300
Gucci	253 Post	27	fine Italian leather goods	772-2539

Shops	Address	Map No.	Description	Telephone
Gumps	250 Post	16	landmark for gifts jade jewels	982-1616
Hastings	101 Post	32	Men & women's haberdashery	393-8900
Helga Howie	133 Kearny	22	Helga designs & Eur access	989-3777
Herbert's Furs	275 Post	26	Variet of designer furs	397-9600
I. Magnin & Co	Stockton/Geary	35	Fine specialty store	362-2100
Jaeger Internatl	272 Post	15	men/women English sports wear	421-3714
Jeffrey Davies	575 Sutter	2	Silk flower arrangements & access	392-1722
Jessica McClintock	353 Sutter	4	Ethereal women's clothes	397-0987
Lane Bryant	55 Geary	40	Clothes for larger sizes	421-4575
Laykin et Cie	Stcktn/Geary	35	Designer Jewelry	362-2100
Louis Vuitton	317 Sutter St	6	Custom leather luggage/access	391-6200
Macy's & Annex	Stcktn/O'Farrell	37	Macy's Best	397-3333
Maison Mendessolle	339 Powell	24	Women's sportswear & accssrs	781-3519
Mark Cross	170 Post	21	Fine jewelry & leathers	391-7770
My Child's Destiny	70 Grant	39	Children's Heaven, tots to teens	397-2424
Neiman Marcus	150 Stockton	36	Fine Specialty Store	362-3900
Orpheus Fashions	309 Sutter	7	Italian Men's habedashery	391-9031
Saks Fifth Ave	384 Post	11	Fine Specialty Store	986-4300
Shreve's	200 Post	19	Jewelry gifts & silver	421-2600
Tiffany & Co	252 Grant	8	jewels silver crystal china	781-7000
Tom Wing & Sons	190 Post	20	Design jewely, jades, antiques	986-5100
Wedgewood SF	304 Stockton	13	collection of china & porcelain	391-5610
Wilkes Bashford	336 Sutter	5	Fine imports for the elegant look	986-4380
Williams-Sonoma	576 Sutter	1	Outstanding culinary collection	982-0295

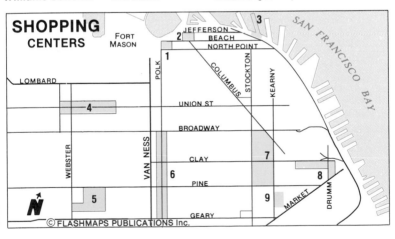

SHOPPING AREAS & CENTERS

Cannery	2	approx 25 specialty shops housed in remodeled Del Monte cannery
Chinatown	7	teakwd ivory porcelains fabrics foodstuffs trinkets over 100 shops
Embarcadero Ctr	8	5 buildings with over 150 shops on 3-level gallery
Galleria at Crocker	9	50 elegant shops in modern 3 level setting
Ghirardelli Sq	1	approx 55 shps & boutiques in remodeled red-brick chocolate factry
Japan Center	5	approx 50 ethnic shops-jewelry/antiques to native food/cookware
Pier 39	3	waterfront shopping complex with 85 food, hobby, variety stores
Polk Street	6	long established merchants lovingly catering to everyday needs
The Anchorage	2	shipboard atmosphere with 50 shops & boutiques
Union Street	4	30 shops in renovated Victorian barns & houses-5 block area

COASTLINE NORTHERN CALIFORNIA
■ **Missions**

Undersea Gardens
(Spectacular underwater viewing of fish and flora)

Redwood National Park
(62,000 forest acres drive along 40 mile coast)

368 ft. Coastal Redwood
(world's tallest tree)

Humboldt Redwoods
(43,000 acres-35-mile "Avenue of the Giants")

Lassen Volcanic Park
(106,000 acres of colorful lava beds, lakes and wilderness)

California Western RR *- "skunk train"*
(40-mile trip thru redwoods along Noyo River)

Mendocino Coast Botanical Garden
(47 acres flowering shrubs on rugged terrain with picnic cliff sites)

Fort Ross — *(Fur trading outpost-1812)*

Point Reyes National Seashore
(65,000 acres of beaches, dunes, lagoons, lighthouse, forests, lakes + 80 miles of foot and bridle trails)

Muir Woods
(550 acres virgin stand of coastal redwoods)

Farallon Islands
(discovered by Juan Rodriguez Cabrillo-1542)

SF Beaches · *(Baker, Ocean & Phelan)*

San Francisco Zoo

Marine World—Africa USA

Big Basin Redwoods
(12,000 acres-trails & natural history museum)

Seventeen—Mile Drive
(Scenic toll route from Pacific Grove to Carmel)

Point Lobos Reserve — *(Cypresses, sea lions, wildflowers)*

Pinnacles National Monument
(Spirelike rock formations & volcanic contours)

Hearst San Simeon State Historic Monument
(Opulent castle, mosaics, art objects, gardens & fine views)

Morro Bay: *(Gibraltar of the Pacific)*

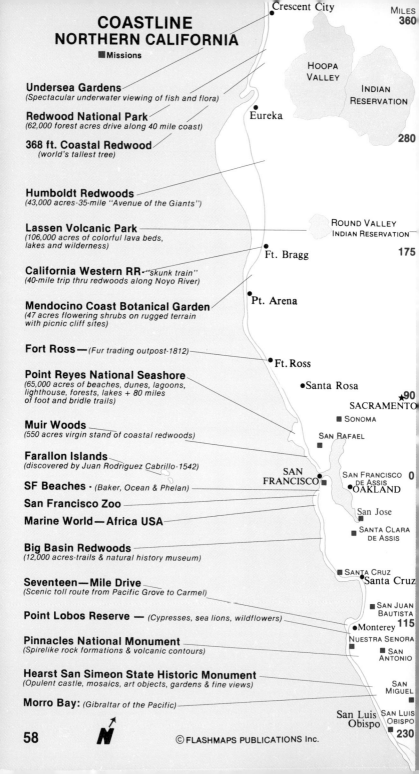

MILES
360

• Crescent City

HOOPA VALLEY

INDIAN RESERVATION

• Eureka

280

ROUND VALLEY
INDIAN RESERVATION

175

• Ft. Bragg

• Pt. Arena

• Ft. Ross

• Santa Rosa

★**90**
SACRAMENTO

■ SONOMA

SAN RAFAEL
■

SAN FRANCISCO • OAKLAND

SAN FRANCISCO DE ASSIS **0**

■ San Jose

■ SANTA CLARA DE ASSIS

■ SANTA CRUZ
• Santa Cruz

■ SAN JUAN BAUTISTA

• Monterey **115**

NUESTRA SENORA
■ SAN ANTONIO

SAN MIGUEL

San Luis Obispo
SAN LUIS OBISPO
■ **230**

N

© FLASHMAPS PUBLICATIONS Inc.

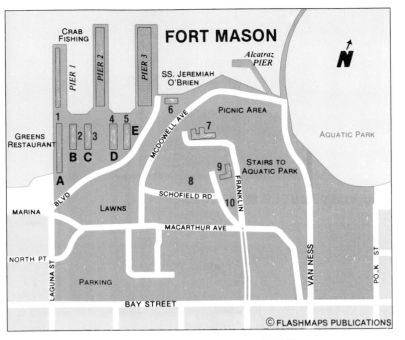

FORT MASON CULTURAL CENTER

CLASSES:	Description	Map No	Telephone
Academy of Media Theater	Ages 12-19 radio, video, film techniques	5	776-4720
Fort Mason Art Center	Sculpture, painting - Day & Night	2	776-8247
Greenpeace	Films, lectures on marine creatures	5	474-6767
Poetry Film Workshop	Classes and Sunday Shows	4	621-3073
Media Alliance	Writing, editing, promotion of literary matter	4	441-2557
Oceanic Society	Lectures, field trips, sailing lessons	5	441-5970
SF Children's Art Council	Ages 2-10, Scholarships available	3	771-0292
Western Public Radio	Writing, production,vocal technique	4	771-1161
MUSEUMS/GALLERIES:			
African-Amer Hist Soc	Library, museum, readings	3	441-0640
Italo-Americano Museum	Exhibits, paintings, sculpture	3	673-2200
Mexican Museum	Folk,colonial,contemp fine art	4	441-0404
Perception Gallery	Varied exhibits	3	776-0347
SF Museum of Modern Art	Large stock of rentals	1	441-4777
World Print Council	Fine Prints-monthly shows	2	776-9200
PERFORMING ARTS:			
Asian American Thea	Folk &ethnic productions	2	928-8922
Magic Theater (2 theaters)	Experimental compny, American & Internat'l	4	441-8001
Music-By-the-Bay	Assist folk musicians-booking,recordng promo	3	474-5600
People's Theater Coalition	Bay Area Theater groups	2	776-8999
Performing Arts Ctr	Readings and critique of new scripts	3	673-2634
Plowshares Coffeehouse	Folk music, American & International	3	441-8910
SF Bay Area Dance Coalition	Dance performances varied groups	3	673-8172
SF Schl Dramatic Art	Repertory group with varied productions	3	885-2766
RECREATION:			
Community Gardens	Free plots to city "gardeners"	8	556-0560
Gamefield	Exercise-walk, game for Senior Citizens	10	556-0560
Historic Houses Walk	Several houses dating from 1850 to 1861	9	556-0560
SF Internat'l Youth Hostel	Bldg 240 130 accommodations; $4 to $6	7	771-7277
Yacht Racing Association	Racing in Bay	3	771-9500

FORT MASON (441-5706) HAS OVER 40 NON-PROFIT ORGANIZATIONS DEDICATED TO
ECOLOGY, HUMANISTIC AND ENVIRONMENTAL STUDIES. ALSO MANY CLASSES FOR CHILDREN.

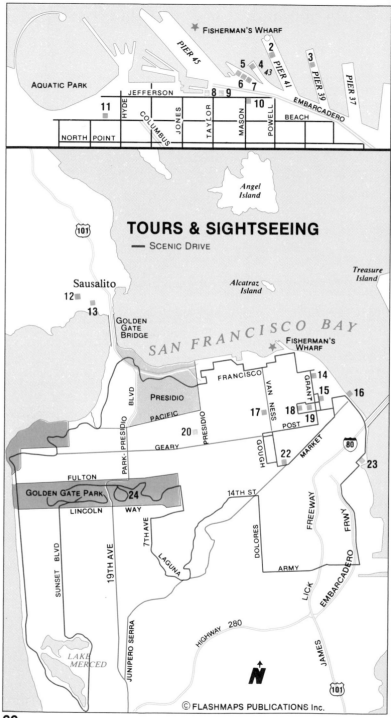

TOURS & SIGHTSEEING
— SCENIC DRIVE

FISHERMAN'S WHARF
PIER 45
PIER 41
PIER 39
PIER 37
2
43
5
4
6
7
8
9
10
11
AQUATIC PARK
JEFFERSON
EMBARCADERO
HYDE
COLUMBUS
JONES
TAYLOR
MASON
POWELL
BEACH
NORTH POINT

Angel Island

Sausalito
12
13
GOLDEN GATE BRIDGE

Alcatraz Island

Treasure Island

SAN FRANCISCO BAY

FISHERMAN'S WHARF
FRANCISCO
Presidio
PARK PRESIDIO BLVD
PACIFIC
PRESIDIO
VAN NESS
GRANT
14
15
16
17
18
19
20
GEARY
GOUGH
POST
MARKET
80
22
23
FULTON
GOLDEN GATE PARK
24
14TH ST
LINCOLN
WAY
7TH AVE
LAGUNA
DOLORES
FREEWAY
EMBARCADERO FRWY
SUNSET BLVD
19TH AVE
JUNIPERO SERRA
ARMY
LICK
HIGHWAY 280
JAMES
LAKE MERCED
N
101

© FLASHMAPS PUBLICATIONS Inc.

EXPLORING BAY AREA BY LAND • SEA • AIR

BY LAND

WALKING TOURS:	Guide*	Address	Map No	Telephone
Bakery	Boudin Sourdough	156 Jefferson	9	928-1849
Chinatown (night)	Ding How Tours	753½ Clay	19	981-8399
Chinese Culture	Chinese Heritage	750 Kearny	15	986-1822
Civic Center	City Guides	666 Filbert	14	558-3981
Coit Tower	City Guides	666 Filbert	14	558-3981
Hall of Flowers	Golden Gate Pk	19th-Lincoln	24	558-3622
Market/No Beach	City Guides	666 Filbert	14	558-3981
Oakland	Oakland Tours	14 Wash St	off map	273-3234
Presidio Army Mus	City Guides	666 Filbert	14	558-3981
Performing Arts	City Guides	Civic Center	14	552-8338
SF Downtown	SF Discovery	1200 Taylor	18	673-2894

BUS TOURS :				
Bay Area	Gray Line	420 Taylor St	22	771-4000
Chinatown (night)	Gray Line	420 Taylor St	22	771-4000
Marin County	Maxi Tours	1961 Chestnut	22	563-2151
Monterey/Carmel	Gray Line	420 Taylor St	22	771-4000
Mt. Tamalpais	Maxi Tours	1961 Chestnut	13	563-2151
Muir Woods	Lorrie's Travel	2660 3rd St	12	826-5950
Oakland-Berkeley	Gray Line	420 Taylor St	off map	771-4000
Sausalito	Lorrie's Travel	2660 3rd St	12	826-5950
San Francisco	Gray Line	420 Taylor St	22	771-4000
	Lorrie's Travel	1660 3rd St	12	826-5950
SF Night Clubs	Gray Line	420 Taylor St	22	771-4000
Wine Country	Gray Line	420 Taylor St	22	771-4000
	Lorrie's Travel	2660 3rd St St	12	826-5950

HISTORIC TOURS :

Architecture	SF Arch Foundation	2007 Franklin	17	441-3046
Balclutha	Maritime Museum	Polk St	11	982-1886
Fire Dept	SF Fire Dept	655 Presidio Av	20	861-8000
Hyde Street Pier	Maritime Mus	Hyde St	11	556-6435
Presidio	U.S. Sixth Army	Bldg 37 Lombard	14	561-3870
San Francisco	Enchntd Wrld SF	Jefferson/Mason	10	885-4834
San Francisco	SF Experience	333 Jefferson St	8	982-7550

BY SEA

Alcatraz Island	Blue & Gold Fleet	Pier 39	3	781-7877
	Harbor Carriers	Pier 41	2	546-2800
	Red & White Fleet	Pier 43½	5	546-2810
Angel Island	Red & White Fleet	Pier 43½	7	546-2810
	Blue & Gold Fleet	Pier 39	3	781-7877
Bay Cruises	Blue & Gold Fleet	Pier 39	3	781-7877
GG & Bay Bridges	Blue & Gold Fleet	Pier 39	3	781-7877
Sausalito	Golden Gate Ferry	Ferry Building	16	982-8834
Tiburon	Blue & Gold Fleet	Pier 39	3	781-7877
	Harbor Tours	Pier 43½	6	546-2815
Treasure Island	Blue & Gold Fleet	Pier 39	3	781-7877

BY AIR

Helicopter	Commodore Heli	Pier 43	4	981-4832
	SF Heli	SF Airport	off map	430-8666

*Call for Tour Times and Group Arrangements
For touring Wine Country and Sonoma farms, see pages 62 and 64.

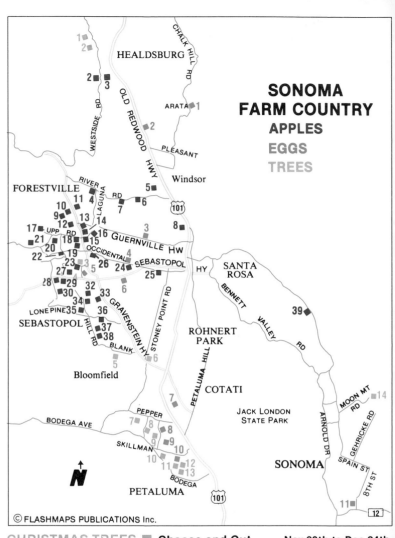

SONOMA
FARM COUNTRY
APPLES
EGGS
TREES

© FLASHMAPS PUBLICATIONS Inc.

62   *Can tag in Nov. by appointment

SONOMA FARMS & ORCHARDS—BY MAP NOS.

APPLES ■ July15th to Nov15th *(depending on variety)*

Grower	Address	Map No.	Other Produce	Telephone Area (707)
Middleton Gardens	2651 Westside Rd	2	6 varieties, + 7 var peaches	433-4755
Hill's Headacres	354 Foreman Lane	3	6 var, + prunes, vegtables	433-3258
Sonshine Acres *	6002 River Road	4	7 var, organic vegetables	838-2274
Stone Ranch	3610 Bisordi Lane	5	Prunes, pears, vegetables	no phone
Cameron Ranch	1175 River Rd	6	squash indian corn pumpkn	546-9319
Martinelli Ranch	3360 River Rd	7	4 var, + pears, vegetables	525-0570
Martin Lambert	3964 Coffey Lane	8	Pears, dried prunes & pears	544-1653
El Molino Farm	9144 Ross Sta Rd	9	Produce, corn in season	887-2532
Kozlowski's Rasbrry	5566 Gravenstein Hy	10	Rasberries, jams, corn, tofu	887-2104
Larson's Keneko *	8500 Templeman Rd	11	strawberry, pear* rasberry*	887-1014
Marcucci Farms	4940 Ross Road	12	pears, jams, walnuts	823-0796
Apple Blossom	4050 Vine Hill Rd	13	6 Varieties	823-6889
Paul Orchards	3561 Gravenstein Hy	15	5 var, + apple juice vegtbls	823-7907
Georgetown Store	4015 Frei Road	16	Pheasant, turkey geese etc	823-9373
Walker Apples	220 Graton Rd	17	23 varieties	823-4310
Hallberg's Farm *	2500 Gravenstein Hy	18	Apple juice, cider	823-2435
Stipinovich Ranch *	9950 O'Connell Rd	18	5 var, picnic area	823-2442
Fogleman Family *	8417 Peachland Ave	19	3 varieties	823-8789
Caswell Winter Crk	13207 Dupont Rd	20	6 var, apple & honey wine	874-2517
Ratzlaff Ranch	13128 Occidental Rd	21	3 var, + Bartlett pears	823-0538
Mill Station Ranch *	9707 Mill Sta Rd	22	4 varieties + Honey	823-8193
Ping Quaw Orchard	8300 Candy Apple Ln	23	6 var, + vegetables, flowers	823-8969
Sanchietti Ranch	1115 Irwin Lane	24	Plums, pears, walnuts	544-5999
Dutton Ranch	2808 Sebastopol Rd	25	Peaches, pears, dried fruits	545-8447
Halle's Apple Ranch	1526 Gravenstein Hy	26	20 var, apple juice	823-4613
Red Shed, The	2195 Pleasant Hill Rd	26	5 var, apple juice	823-6018
George LeBallister	9180 Bodega Hwy	27	All Varieties, + sweet corn	823-0416
Bill's Farm Basket	10315 Bodega Hwy	28	Peaches, melons, vegtbles	829-1777
Apple Tree	10055 Bodega Hwy	29	4 Varieties	823-3605
S. DeVoto Orchard	1165 Gold Ridge Rd	29	9 var, dried/fresh flowerss	823-6650
Vista Del Valle *	1045 Sexton Road	30	8 var, + pears, persimmons +	823-9538
Voge Ten Fruit Stnd	1430 Hollman Lane	32	Figs peaches persimmons +	823-0485
Twin Hill Ranch *	1689 Pleasant Hill rd	33	Cherries nuts dried fruit +	823-2815
Frank's Apple Stand	1794 Gravenstein Hy	34	cider squash walnts cherries	829-1106
Marshall Apple	8030 Kennedy Road	35	4 Varieties	823-0477
Buena Vista *	1200 Cunningham Rd	36	10 var bring contners + cider	823-9613
Snyder Ranch *	1890 Schaeffer Rd	37	Cherries 10 var. 6/13-7/16	823-9300
Stokes Ranch	1910 Schaeffer Rd	38	Pears and plums	823-8285
Indian Springs	740 Lawndale Rd	39	4 var, apple juice	833-2089

*You can pick

EGGS ■ Open all year *(check days and time)*

Farm or Ranch	Address	Map No.	Poultry and Such	Telephone (707)
Rocking W A Ranch	12000 Chalk Hill Rd	1	Turkeys, beef, pork, lamb	433-3261
Johnson Egg Farm	259 Arata Lane	2	Chicken manure, goats	838-2429
Sunnyside Farms	2971 Guerneville Rd	3	Cheese, brkfast meats, milk	542-3332
D. Grossi Ranch	4993 Occidental Rd	4	Chickens, walnuts, honey	542-2604
Buzzard's Roost	1778 Facendini Ln	5	fryers, turkeys, yarns	823-2799
Chicken Crossing	1100 Ozone Dr	5	Fertile brown & live chickens	575-8917
Willie Bird Turkey	6350 Hwy 12	6	Fresh & smoked poultry	545-2832
Redwood Egg Farm	10029 Minnesota Ave	7	11 grades of eggs	795-5828
Liberty Farms	395 Liberty Road	8	Eggs only	795-8937
Miller Ranch Store	700 Cavanaugh Lane	9	Eggs only	763-0921
Sikora's Geese	747 Marshall Ave	10	7 breeds of geese, goslings	762-1315

63

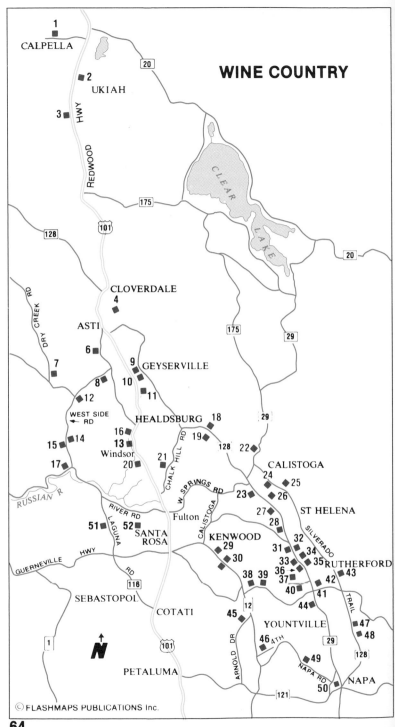

WINE COUNTRY—ALPHABETICAL
(Napa • Sonoma • Mendocino Counties)

Winery	Address	Approx miles from SF	Map No.	Vineyard Favorites	(Area 707) Telephone
Adler Fels	5325 Corrick Rd	62	29	Chardonnay,Fume Blanc	539-3123
Alexander Valley	8644 Hwy 128	75	18	Riesling,Cabernet Sauv	433-7209
Beaulieu	1960 St Helena	63	41	Chardonnay,Cabernet Sauv	963-2411
Beringer	2000 Main St	66	28	Chardonnay,Cabernet Sauv	963-7115
Buena Vista	18000 OldWnery	60	39	Zinfandel,Johannisberg	938-1266
Chateau Montelena	1429 Tubbs Ln	80	22	Chardonnay,Cabernet Sauv	942-5105
Chateau St Jean	8555 Sonoma Rd	60	29	Chardonnay,Johannisberg	833-4134
Christian Brothers	255 N Main St	65	50	Pinot Chardonnay Zinfandel	963-2719
Clos du Val	5330 Silverado	65	47	Zinfandel,Cabernet Sauv	252-6711
Cresta Blanca	2399 N State	100	2	Gewurztraminer,Zinfandel	462-2985
Cuvaison	550 Silverado	75	25	Chardonnay,Cabernet Sauv	942-6266
Davis Bynum	8075 Westside	70	15	Fume Blanc,Pinot Noir	433-5852
Domaine Chandon	California Drive	60	27	Blanc de Noir,Napa Vlly Brut	944-2280
Dry Creek	Lambert Bridge	80	12	Fume Blanc,Zinfandel	433-1000
Fetzer	D'twn Hopland	100	3	Gamay Beaujls,Cabernet Sau	744-1737
Foppiano	12707 OldRdwd	70	16	Petite Sirah,Chardonnay	433-7272
Geyser Peak	22281 Chianti	85	6	Gewurztraminer,Chardonnay	433-6585
Glen Ellen	1883 London Rnc	55	45	Chardonnay,Sauv Blanc	996-1066
Grand Cru	1 Vintage Ln	60	30	Gewurztraminer,Chenin Bl	996-8100
Grgich Hills	1829 St Helena	67	36	Chardonnay,Zinfandel	963-2784
Gundlach-Bundschu	2000Denmark	50	49	Merlot,Chardonnay	938-5277
Hacienda	1000 Vineyard Ln	60	38	Chardonnay,Chenin Blanc	938-3220
Hanns Kornell	1091 Larkmead	75	26	Sehr Trocken,Dry Champagne	963-2334
Heitz	436 St Helena	67	34	Chardonnay,Cabernet Sauv	963-3542
Hop Kiln	6050 Westside	70	14	Zinfandel,Johannisberg	433-6491
Inglenook	St Helena Hwy	67	37	Charbono,Johnnsbrg Rsl	963-7184
Iron Horse	9786 Ross Sta	58	51	Pinot Noir,Sparkling wine	887-1507
ItalianSwissColony	26150 Asti Rd	80	4	Zinfandel,Chenin Blanc	433-2333
Johnson's	8333 Hy 128	75	19	Pinot Noir,Cabernet Sauv	433-2319
Jordan	1474 Alexndr Val	76	11	Chardonnay,Cabernet Sauv	433-6955
Kenwood	9592 Sonoma	60	30	Chardonnay,Cabernet Sauv	833-5891
Korbel Cellars	13250 River Rd	73	17	Nat Chmpgne,Chablis	887-2294
Landmark	9150 Los Amigos	65	21	Chardonnay,Cabernet Sauv	838-9466
Louis M Martini	St Helena Hy S	68	32	Zinfandel,Barbera	963-2736
Mondavi, Robert	7801 St Helena S	65	40	Fume Blanc,Cabernet Sauv	963-9611
Nervo	19550Geyserville	75	9	Farmers Table,WinterChill	857-3417
Parducci	501 Farducci Rd	100	1	FrColombard,Gamay Beauj	462-3828
Pedroncelli, J.	1220 Canyon Rd	75	7	Zinfandel,Cabernet Sauv	857-3619
Piper Sonoma	11447 Old Redwd	21	13	Brut	433-8843
Rodney Strong/Wnd	11455OldRedwd	65	20	Chardonnay,Petite Sirah	433-6511
Rutherford Vintners	1673 St Helena S	68	33	Johannisbrg Rslng,Cabernet	963-4117
Schramsberg	St Helena Hy	75	23	Blanc deNoir,Cuvee Pinot	942-4558
Sebastiani	389-4th St E	50	46	Barbera,Cabernet Sauvign	938-5532
Simi	16275Healdsbrg	75	11	Chardonnay,Cabernet Sauv	433-6981
Sonoma-Cutrer	4401 Slusser	60	52	Chardonnay	528-1181
Souverain	IndependenceLn	75	8	FumeBlanc,Cabernet Sauv	433-6918
Stags Leap	5766 Silverado	70	43	Merlot, Johannisberg RsIng	944-2782
Sterling	1111 Dunweal	75	24	Merlot,Chardonnay	942-5151
Sutter Home	277 St Helena S	68	31	Amador conty WhZinfandel	963-3104
Trefethen	1160 Oak Knoll	60	48	Chardonnay,Pinot Noir	255-7700
Trentadue	19170 Redwood	75	10	Carignane,Zinfandel	433-3104
V. Sattui	White Lane	68	35	Zinfandel,Johannisberg	963-7774

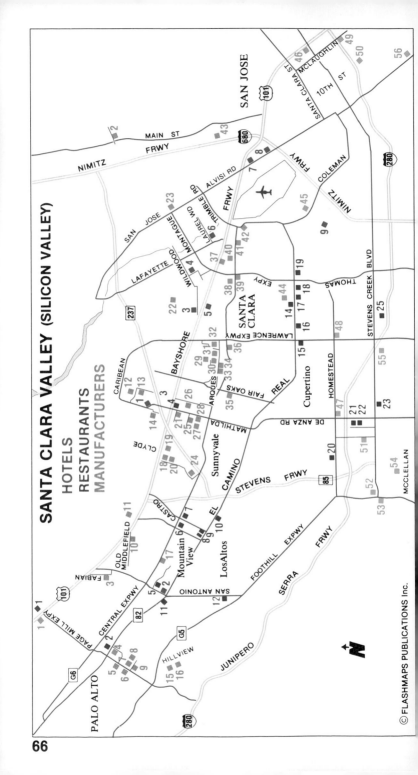

SANTA CLARA AREA

VALLEY HOTELS

Hotel	Address	Map No	Area (408) Telephone	Rooms
Hilton Sunnyvale	1250 Lakeside, Sunnyvale	5	738-4888	305
Holiday Inn	1217 Wildwood Wy, Sunnyvale	3	245-5330	180
Hyatt, Rickey's	4219 El Camino, Palo Alto	2	493-8000	350
Hyatt San Jose	1740 N 1st, San Jose	7	298-0300	500
Le Baron	1350 N 1st, San Jose	8	288-9200	350
Los Gatos	50 Saratoga Ave, San Jose	9	354-3300	127
Marriott	2700 Mission Coll, Santa Clara	4	988-1500	760
Ramada Inn	2151 Laurelwood, Santa Clara	6	988-8411	130
Sheraton Inn	1100 N Matilda, Sunnyvale	1	745-6000	174

VALLEY RESTAURANTS

Restaurant	Address	Map No.	Cuisine	Average Price	(408) - *(415) Telephone
Acapulco	1299 Lawrence Exp	15	Mexican	$5-12	249-2001
Anthony's Pier 9	10745 N De Anza	22	Seafd/Ital	10-20	255-4711
Au Chambertin	170 State St	12	Fr/Continent	10-20	*948-8721
Augusto's	856 El Camino Real	8	Continental	10-20	*965-1869
Bacchus Inn	2825 El Camino Real	14	French/Ital	7-15	296-8328
Bewon	3430 El Camino Real	16	Korean	7-15	244-5020
Bourbon Street	2540 California	5	Creole	15-20	*941-4433
Brandywine Room	Hilton Sunnyvale	13	Continental	10-15	738-4888
Encore	833 W El Camino Real	9	French	10-15	245-2345
Fish Market	3775 El Camino Real	2	Seafood	6-12	246-3474
Florentine	118 Castro, Mt View	7	Italian	6-12	961-6543
Gifu	20625 Alves Ave	25	Japanese	10-20	252-6460
Hamasushi	20030 Stevens Crk	23	Japanese	7-17	446-4262
Hugo's	Hyatt San Jose	24	Continental	18-25	298-0300
La Paloma	2280 El Camino Real	19	Mexican	5-10	247-0990
Le Pavilion	Le Baron Hotel	8	Continental	25+	288-9200
Machado	2460 El Camino Real	18	Portuguese	10-20	296-4144
Marquis French	2800 El Camino Real	17	Continental	10-20	248-7866
Monterey Whaling	190 E El Camino Real	10	Seafood	9-15	*969-4323
Ming's	1700 Embarcadero	1	Chinese	15-20	856-7700
Mui Kiang	895 Villa St	6	Hakka	10-20	*969-8232
Rodeo	1108 N Matilda	3	American	10-15	745-6214
Rong Shing	10725 N De Anza	21	Szechuan	8-20	252-3398
Ruby King	4320 El Camino Real	11	Cantonese	6-15	*941-1167
Victoria Station	855 E Homestead	20	Steak	10-20	739-7670

MAJOR SANTA CLARA MANUFACTURERS (Silicon Valley)

Company	Map No.	Company	Map No.	Company	Map No.
Acurex	19	Fairchild Cameras Instr.	18	Nat'l Semiconductor	36
Advanced Micro	29	Ford Motor Co	2	Owens-Corning Fiber.	41
Amdahl Corp.	32	Ford Aerospace Comm.	3	Precision Monolithics	37
Amer Microsystems	48	Four Phase Systems	47	Raytheon Semicon.	20
Apple Computer	51	GTE Systems	24	Rolm Corporation	22
Aplied Technology	21	General Electric	56	San Jose Mercury Nws	43
Argosystems	11	Hewlett-Packard	6	San Jose Steel	46
Atari Inc.	13	ISS Sperry Univac	40	Signetics Corporation	33
Beckman Instruments	1	Intel Corporation	44	Singer-Link Division	34
Burke Industries	50	Intersil Inc.	55	Spectra-Physics	10
Chemical Systems	30	ITT Jennings	49	Synertek Inc.	38
Coherent Inc.	7	Kaiser Aluminum	52	Syntex Corporation	16
Container Corp	42	Kaiser Cement	53	Tab Products	8
Cushman Electronics	23	Kodak Processing Lab	5	Teledyne M.E.C.	9
Data General	28	Lockheed Missiles	14	TRW-Vidar Division	17
Eaton Corporation	27	Measurex	54	Varian Associates	4
ATC Med Tech	25	Memorex	39	Versatec Inc.	44
ESL Inc.	12	Monolithic Memories	31	Watkins-Johnson	15
FMC Corporation	45	NCR Corporation	26	Westinghouse Electron.	35

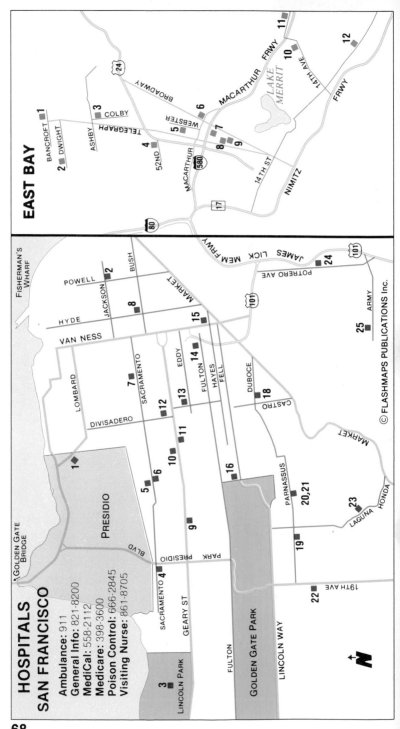

HOSPITALS
SAN FRANCISCO

Ambulance: 911
General Info: 821-8200
MediCal: 558-2112
Medicare: 398-3600
Poison Control: 666-2845
Visiting Nurse: 861-8705

© FLASHMAPS PUBLICATIONS Inc.

EAST BAY

HOSPITALS—SAN FRANCISCO & OAKLAND

SAN FRANCISCO
1 Letterman Army
2 Chinese
3 Veteran's Admin
5 Marshal Hale
6 Children's
7 Presbyterian
8 St. Francis
9 French
10 Garden-Sullivan
10 Pacific Medical
11 Kaiser Foundation
12 Mount Zion

13 Calif Podiatry
15 SF Community
16 St. Mary's
18 Davies/Franklin
19 Langley Porter
20 H. C. Moffit
21 U of Calif Med
22 Shriners
23 Laguna Honda
24 SF General
25 St. Luke's

OAKLAND
1 Cowell, Ernest
2 Herrick
3 Alta Bates
4 Children's
5 Women's
6 Kaiser Foundation
7 Merritt, Samuel
8 Peralta
9 Providence
10 Highland General
11 Naval Regional
12 Oakland

HOSPITALS—ALPHABETICAL

SAN FRANCISCO

	Address	Map No.	Telephone
California Podiatry	1210 Scott Street	13	563-3444
Children's Hospital of S. F.	3700 California St	6	387-8700
Chinese	845 Jackson St	2	982-2400
Franklin Hospital	Castro & Duboce Sts	18	565-6779
French	4131 Geary Blvd	9	386-9000
Garden Sullivan(Pacific Med Ctr)	2750 Geary Blvd	10	921-6171
H. C. Moffitt-U of Calif	3rd & Parnassus	20	666-9000
Kaiser Foundation	2425 Geary Blvd	11	929-4000
Laguna Honda Hosp & Rehab	375 Laguna Honda	23	664-1580
Langley Porter Neuropsychiatric	401 Parnassus Ave	19	681-8080
Letterman Army Medical Center	Presidio	1	561-2231
Marshall Hale Memorial	3773 Sacramento St	5	386-7000
Mount Zion Medical Center	1600 Divisadero St	12	567-6600
Pacific Medical Center	2750 Geary Blvd	10	921-6171
Presbyterian	2333 Buchanan	7	563-4321
Ralph K Davies Med Ctr	Castro & Duboce Sts	18	565-6779
San Francisco Community Mental	101 Grove St	15	387-5100
San Francisco General	1001 Potrero	24	821-8200
St. Francis Memorial	900 Hyde St	8	775-4321
St. Luke's	3555 Army Street	25	647-8600
St. Mary's Medical Center	450 Stanyon	16	668-1000
Shriners Hosp Crippled Children	1701 19th Ave	22	665-1100
Univ of Calif Medical Center	3rd & Parnassus Ave	21	666-9000
Veterans Admin Med Center	4150 Clement St	3	221-4810

OAKLAND

	Address	Map No.	Telephone
Alta Bates	3001 Colby St, Berkeley	3	540-0337
Childrens Hosp Med Ctr No CA	747 52nd St	4	428-3000
Cowell, Ernest V Memorial	Univ of CA, Berkeley	1	642-2000
Herrick Health Center	2001 Dwight Wy, Berkeley	2	845-0130
Highland General	1411 E. 31st	10	534-8055
Kaiser Foundation	280 W MacArthur Blvd	6	428-5000
Merritt, Samuel	Hawthorne & Webster	7	655-4000
Naval Regional Med Center	8750 Mountain Blvd	11	633-5000
Oakland	2648 E 14th St	12	532-3300
Peralta	450 30th Street	8	451-4900
Providence	3100 Summit St	9	835-4500
Women's Hospital	400 40th St	5	652-6503

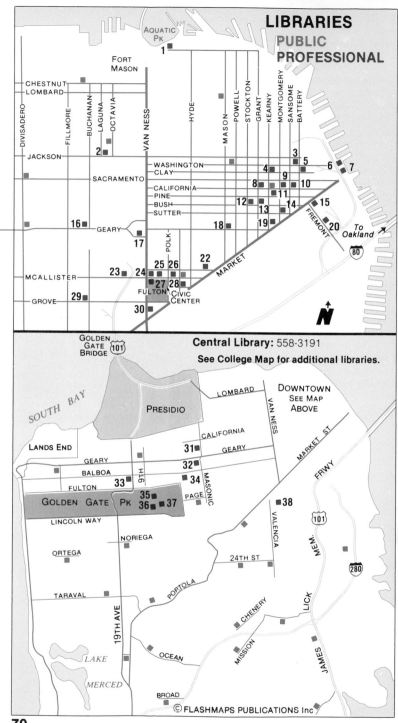

LIBRARIES

PUBLIC
PROFESSIONAL

Central Library: 558-3191

See College Map for additional libraries.

PROFESSIONAL LIBRARIES—ALPHABETICAL

Library	Address	Map No	Telephone
African-American Society	680 McAllister St	23	441-0640
American Indian	1451 Masonic Ave	32	626-5235
American Merchant Marine	Pier 1½	6	788-3942
American Russian Institute	90 McAllister Street	22	753-6355
Archives of American Art	De Young Museum	35	556-2530
Avery Brundage Collection	Asian Art Museum	35	558-2993
Bank of America	555 California St-6th Fl	11	622-2068
British Consulate General	120 Montgomery St	14	981-3030
California Academy of Sciences	Golden Gate Park	37	221-4214
California Automible Assoc (AAA)	150 Van Ness	30	565-2300
California Div Mines & Geology	Ferry Bldg Rm 2022	7	671-4941
California Historical Society	2090 Jackson St	2	567-1848
Canadian Consulate	1 Maritime Place	5	981-2670
Chinese Culture	750 Kearny Street	4	986-1822
City Planning Library	450 McAllister St	28	558-3055
Far West Lab Womens Ed	1855 Folsom Street	38	565-3000
Federal Information Center	450 Golden Gate Ave	26	556-6600
Federal Reserve Bank-SF Resrch	101 Market St	9	392-6640
Fireman's Fund	3333 California St	31	929-2000
French Library	414 Mason	18	781-8755
Goethe Institute	530 Bush St	13	391-0370
Internatl Longshoremen's Union	1188 Franklin St	17	775-0533
Japanese Information Services	1737 Post St	16	989-7140
Jewish Community Library	639 14th Avenue	33	751-6983
Mechanics Institute	57 Post St	19	421-1750
Nat'l Maritime Shaw Library	Foot of Polk St	1	556-8177
National Park Service	450 Golden Gate Ave	26	556-4165
Paulist Library	614 Grant-Old St. Mary's	8	362-0959
Russell Library of Horticulture	Strybing Arboretum	36	661-1316
SF County Law	400 Van Ness Ave	27	558-4627
SF Lighthouse Center	745 Buchanan St	29	431-1481
SF Room & Archive	Main Lib-3rd fl, Civic Center	26	558-3949
Sierra Club-Colby Memorial	500 Bush St	12	981-8634
Sloss Ackerman Fine Arts	SF Mus of Modern Art	24	863-8800
Society of California Pioneers	456 McAllister St	25	861-5278
Sutro Library	2495 Golden Gate Ave	34	731-4477
US Dept of Energy	333 Market 7th Fl	15	974-7038
US Dept Labor Statistics	450 Golden Gate 10th Fl	26	556-4678
US Environmental Protection	215 Fremont St	20	974-8071
US Geological Survey	555 Battery St	3	556-5627
Wells Fargo	475 Sansome	10	396-5744

PROFESSIONAL LIBRARIES—BAY AREA

Library	Address	Telephone
Asian Community	449 9th St, Oakland	273-3400
Bancroft Collection	Univ of California, Berkeley	642-3403
BART Mass Transportation	800 Madison Street, Oakand	464-6000
Chevron Research Co	576 Standard Ave, Richmnd	620-3000
Data Center	464 19th Street, Oakland	835-4692
Doe Memorial (Main)	Univ of California, Berkeley	642-6657
Earthquake Engineer Research	47th & Hoffman Street, Richmond	231-9403
Film Archives	Univ Calif Art Museum, Berkeley	642-1124
Institute Gov Studies	109 Moses Hall U Calif, Berkeley	642-1472
Latin American	1900 Fruitvale Ave, Oakland	532-7882
Oakland Genealogical	4780 Lincoln Avenue, Oakland	531-3905
Oakland Central	125 14th Street, Oakland	273-3134
Western Jewish Center	Judah Magnes Museum, Oakland	849-2710

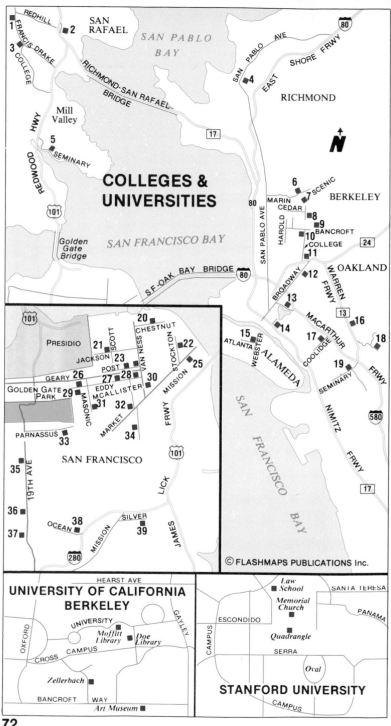

COLLEGES & UNIVERSITIES

SAN RAFAEL

SAN PABLO BAY

REDHILL

FRANCIS DRAKE

COLLEGE

RICHMOND-SAN RAFAEL BRIDGE

Mill Valley

SEMINARY

REDWOOD HWY

101

Golden Gate Bridge

SAN FRANCISCO BAY

SF-OAK BAY BRIDGE

80

SAN PABLO AVE

EAST SHORE FRWY

RICHMOND

17

80

SAN PABLO AVE

MARIN

CEDAR

HAROLD

COLLEGE

SCENIC

BERKELEY

BANCROFT

24

OAKLAND

BROADWAY

WARREN FRWY

MACARTHUR

13

COOLIDGE

SEMINARY

NIMITZ FRWY

580

17

ATLANTA

WEBSTER

ALAMEDA

SAN FRANCISCO BAY

101

PRESIDIO

SCOTT

CHESTNUT

JACKSON

VAN NESS

STOCKTON

GEARY

POST

EDDY

MCALLISTER

MISSION

FRWY

Golden Gate Park

MASONIC

MARKET

PARNASSUS

SAN FRANCISCO

19TH AVE

OCEAN

MISSION

SILVER

JAMES

LICK

101

280

© FLASHMAPS PUBLICATIONS Inc.

UNIVERSITY OF CALIFORNIA BERKELEY

HEARST AVE

OXFORD

UNIVERSITY

GAYLEY

Moffitt Library

Doe Library

CROSS

CAMPUS

Zellerbach

BANCROFT WAY

Art Museum

STANFORD UNIVERSITY

Law School

SANTA TERESA

Memorial Church

ESCONDIDO

PANAMA

CAMPUS

Quadrangle

SERRA

Oval

CAMPUS

COLLEGES & UNIVERSITIES—BY MAP NO.

1 SF Theological Seminary
2 Dominican College San Rafael
3 Marin College
4 Contra Costa College
5 Golden Gate Baptist Theology
6 Pacific Lutheran Theological
7 Pacific School of Religion
8 Graduate Theological Union
8 Starr King School for Ministry
9 Univ of California-Berkeley
10 Armstrong College
11 St. Albert College
12 Calif College Arts & Crafts
13 Peralta Junior College
14 Laney College
15 College of Alameda
16 Holy Names, College of
17 Patten Bible College
18 Merritt College
19 Mills College
20 San Francisco Art Institute

21 Music & Arts Institute
22 Cogswell Polytechnical
23 SF College Mortuary Science
25 Heald Institute Technology
25 Golden Gate University
26 Lone Mountain Campus (Univ SF)
27 California Podiatry
28 Heald Business College
29 San Francisco University
30 Hastings College of Law
31 Lincoln University
32 U of California Extension
33 Calif of SF Medical
34 New College of California
35 SF Conservatory Music
36 Calif Institute Integral Studies
37 Calif State Univ of SF
38 SF City College
39 Simpson College
40 Stanford University

COLLEGES & UNIVERSITIES—ALPHABETICAL

College	Address	Map No.	Telephone
Armstrong College	2222 Harold Way, Berkeley	10	848-2500
California College Arts & Crafts	B'way & College, Oakland	12	653-8118
Calif Instit Integral Studies	3494 21st Avenue	36	648-1489
California Podiatry	1835 Ellis St	27	563-3444
Calif State Univ SF	1600 Holloway Ave	37	469-2141
California Univ of SF Medical	501 Parnassus Ave	33	666-9000
California Univ Extension Ctr	55 Laguna St	32	642-4111
California Univ at Berkeley	Bancroft-Le Conte, Berkeley	9	642-6000
Cogswell Polytechnical	600 Stockton Street	22	433-5550
College of Alameda	555 Atlantic, Alameda	15	522-7221
Contra Costa	2600 Mission Bell, San Pablo	4	235-7800
Dominican College San Rafael	1520 Grand, San Rafael	2	457-4440
Golden Gate Baptist Theo	Seminary Dr, Mill Valley	5	388-8080
Golden Gate University	536 Mission	25	442-7000
Graduate Theological Union	2465 Le Conte, Berkeley	8	841-9811
Hastings Col Law, U of C	198 McAllister St	30	557-1950
Heald Institute of Technology	150 Fourth Street	25	441-5555
Heald Business College	1188 Franklin	28	673-5500
Holy Names, College of	3500 Mtn. Blvd, Oakland	16	436-0111
Laney College	900 Fallon, Oakland	14	834-5740
Lincoln University	281 Masonic Avenue	31	221-1212
Lone Mountain (Univ SF)	2800 Turk Blvd	26	666-6886
Marin College	College Ave, Kentfield	3	457-8811
Merritt College	12500 Campus Dr., Oakland	18	531-4911
Mills College	Seminary-MacArthur, Oakland	19	430-2255
Music & Arts Institute	2622 Jackson St	21	567-1445
New College of Calif.	777 Valencia Street	34	626-1694
Pacific Lutheran Theo	2770 Marin Ave, Berkeley	6	524-5264

COLLEGES & UNIVERSITIES Continued

College	Address	Map No.	Telephone
Pacific School of Religion	1798 Scenic Ave, Berkeley	7	848-0528
Patten Bible College	2433 Coolidge Ave, Oakland	17	533-8300
Peralta Junior College	333 E 8th St, Oakland	13	466-7200
St. Albert College	5890 Birch Ct., Oakland	11	849-2030
S. F. Art Institute	800 Chestnut St	20	771-7020
S. F. City College of	50 Phelan Ave	38	239-3380
S. F. College Mortuary Science	1450 Post St	23	567-0674
S. F. Conservatory Music	1201 Ortega St	35	564-8086
S. F. State University	1600 Holloway Ave	37	469-2141
S. F. Theological Seminary	2 Kensington, San Anselmo	1	453-2280
S. F. University of	Golden Gate & Barker Ave	29	666-6886
San Mateo College	1700 Hillsdale, San Mateo	22	574-6500
Simpson College	801 Silver Ave	39	334-7400
Stanford University	300 Pasteur Dr., Palo Alto	40	497-2300
Starr King School Ministry	2441 Le Conte Ave, Berkeley	8	845-6232

COLLEGES & UNIVERSITIES SAN FRANCISCO AREA

College	Address	Approx Dist from SF	Telephone
California Maritime Acad	P.O. 1392, Vallejo	31	(707) 644-5601
California State U-Hayward	25800 Hillary St, Hayward	21	881-3000
California State-Sonoma	1801 E Cotati, Rohnert Pk	44	(707) 664-2880
Canada College	4200 Farmhill, Redwood City	29	364-1212
Chabot College	25555 Hesperian, Hayward	33	786-6600
College of Notre Dame	Ralston Ave, Belmont	24	593-1601
De Anza College	21250 Stevens Cr, Cupertino	42	(408) 996-4720
Diablo Valley	321 Golf Club, Pleasant Hill	28	685-1230
Evergreen Valley College	3095 Yerba Buena, San Jose	50	(408) 274-7900
Foothill College	12345 El Monte, Los Altos	31	960-4600
Indian Valley College	1800 Ignacio Blvd, Novato	31	883-2211
John F Kennedy Univ	12 Altarinda Dr, Orinda	15	254-0200
Los Medanos	2700 E Leland, Pittsburg	40	439-2181
Marin College	801 College Ave, Kentfield	18	457-8811
Menlo College	El Camino Real, Atherton	30	323-6141
Mission College	3000 Mission Blvd, Santa Clara	48	(408) 988-2200
Napa College	2277 Napa-Vallejo Hwy	41	(707) 253-3095
Ohlone College	43600 Mission, Fremont	35	659-6000
Pacific Union College	Angwin, Calif	68	(707) 965-6336
St. Mary's of Calif	St Mary's Way, Moraga	19	376-4411
St. Joseph's College	P.O. 151, Mountain View	43	967-9501
San Jose City College	2100 Moorpark, San Jose	50	(408) 298-2181
San Jose State	125 S 7th St, San Jose	50	(408) 277-3228
San Mateo College	1700 Hillsdale, San Mateo	18	574-6161
Skyline College	3300 College Dr, San Bruno	11	355-7000
Solano Community	4000 Suisun Val, Suisun City	42	(707) 864-7000
Univ Santa Clara	Alameda Blvd, San Jose	48	(408) 554-4764
World College West	88 Belvedere, San Rafael	19	332-4522
Wright Institute	2728 Durant Ave, Berkeley	12	841-9230

CIVIC CENTER

Building	Address	Map No	Telephone
Art Commission	165 Grove Street	**15**	558-3463
Board of Education	135 Van Ness Avenue	**18**	565-9000
Brooks Hall	Civic Ctr Plz, 99 Grove (underground)	**10**	626-5010
City Hall ★	Grove & Polk Streets	**9**	558-6161

First Floor

Department	Room	Telephone
CIVIL SERVICE	151	558-4495
CONTROLLER	109	558-4294
JURY COMMISSION	165	558-5617
MAYOR'S CITIZENS CTR	160	558-2666
PERMIT APPEALS BD	154A	558-4421
RECORDER (OFFICIAL)	167	558-3493
PRINCIPAL CLERK	167	558-3494
REAL ESTATE INFO	107	558-3451
SMALL CLAIMS	164	558-3211
TAX ASSESSOR	101	558-3931
TAX COLLECTOR	107	558-3761
PERMITS FOR BUSINESS, DOGS AND PARKING		
TREASURER	110	558-4575
VOTER REGISTRATION	158	558-3417

Second Floor

Department	Room	Telephone
BOARD OF SUPERVISORS	235	558-3184
CHIEF ADMINISTRATOR	289	558-4851
CITY ATTORNEY	206	558-3315
DIRECTOR PUBLIC WORKS	260	558-3671
MAYOR'S OFFICE	200	558-3456
PUBLIC UTILITIES COM	289	558-4986

Third & Fourth Floor

Department	Room	Telephone
MUNICIPAL COURT	8 RMS	558-4041
CLERK OF COURT	300	558-4041
COUNTY CLERK	317	558-2823
SHERIFF	333	558-2411
SUPERIOR COURT	20 RMS	558-3261
CLERK OF COURT	480	558-4311
LAW LIBRARY	436	558-4869

Building	Address	Map No	Telephone
City Hall Annex	450 McAllister Street	**4**	558-6161
BUILDING PERMITS: 558-3294 ELECTRIC INSPECTION: 861-7363 PLUMBING INSPECTION: 861-6402			
City Planning Dept	100 Larkin Street	**12**	558-2151
Civic Auditorium	Grove & Polk Streets	**17**	974-4000
Davies Symphony Hall	Grove & Van Ness	**14**	431-5400
HERBST THEATER · TELEPHONE: 431-5400			
Federal Bldg/Courthouse	450 Golden Gate Ave	**1**	556-3031
Fire Department Hdqtrs	260 Golden Gate Ave	**2**	861-8000
Hastings College Law	200 McAllister Street	**6**	557-0448
Health Center	101 Grove Street	**16**	558-2896
Old Federal Bldg	50 United Nations Plaza	**13**	556-1300
SF Ballet	455 Franklin Street	**A8**	861-5600
SF Main Library	Civic Center	**11**	558-3191
Society of Calif Pioneers	456 McAllister Street	**3**	861-5278
State Building	350 McAllister Street	**5**	(916) 322-9900
Veterans Building	Van Ness at McAllister	**7**	621-6600
SF MUSEUM OF MODERN ART LOCATED ON TOP FLOOR. TELEPHONE: 863-8800			
War Mem Opera House	Van Ness & Grove	**8**	864-3330

★ Hall of Justice · 850 Bryant Street · POLICE DEPT HDQTRS, PUBLIC DEFENDER, DISTRICT ATTORNEY, CORONER, CRIMINAL COURTROOMS, TRAFFIC FINES.

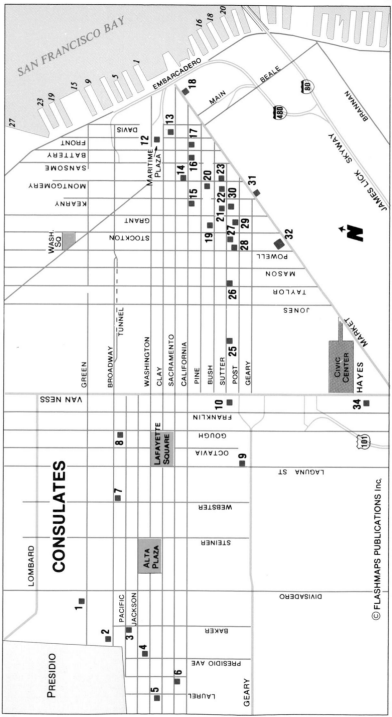

CONSULATES

SAN FRANCISCO BAY

© FLASHMAPS PUBLICATIONS Inc.

76

CONSULATES—ALPHABETICAL

Consulate	Address	Map No.	Telephone
Argentina	870 Market Street	32	982-3050
Australia	360 Post Street	28	362-6160
Austria	256 Sutter Street	21	986-4040
Belgium	999 Sutter Street	25	474-4800
Bolivia	870 Market Street	32	495-5173
Brazil	300 Montgomery Street	14	981-8170
Canada	1 Maritime Plaza	12	981-2670
Chile	870 Market Street	32	982-7662
China People's Rep.	1450 Laguna Street	9	563-4885
Colombia	870 Market Street	32	362-0080
Costa Rica	209 Post Street	30	392-8488
Denmark	1 Market Place	18	781-1309
Dominican Republic	870 Market Street	32	982-5144
Ecuador	870 Market Street	32	391-4148
El Salvador	870 Market Street	32	781-7924
Egypt	3001 Pacific Avenue	3	346-9700
Finland	120 Montgomery	23	981-4656
France	540 Bush Street	19	397-4330
Germany	601 California	15	981-4250
Great Britain	120 Montgomery	23	981-3030
Greece	2441 Gough	8	775-2102
Guatemala	870 Market Street	32	781-0118
Honduras	870 Market Street	32	392-0076
Indonesia	351 California	17	982-8966
Ireland	681 Market Street	31	392-4214
Israel	693 Sutter Street	26	775-5535
Italy	2590 Webster	7	931-4924
Japan	Post & Laguna	9	921-8000
Korea	3500 Clay Street	5	921-2251
Liberia	2950 Broadway	2	921-7869
Malaysia	2 Embarcadero Center	13	421-6570
Mexico	870 Market Street	32	392-5554
Monaco	425 California	16	362-5050
Netherlands	601 California	15	981-6454
New Zealand	1 Maritime Plaza	12	788-7430
Nigeria	369 Hayes Street	34	864-8001
Norway	2 Embarcadero Center	13	986-0766
Pakistan	211 Sutter Street	30	788-0677
Panama	870 Market Street	32	989-0934
Paraguay	870 Market Street	32	982-9424
Peru	870 Market Street	32	362-5185
Philippines	447 Sutter Street	27	433-6666
Portugal	3298 Washington	4	346-3400
Soviet Union	2790 Green Street	1	922-6642
Sweden	120 Montgomery	23	788-2631
Switzerland	235 Montgomery	20	788-2272
Tunisia	3401 Sacramento	6	922-9222
Uruguay	870 Market Street	32	982-3730
Venezuela	870 Market Street	32	421-5172
Yemen Arab Rep	120 Montgomery	23	989-3636
Yugoslavia	1375 Sutter Street	10	776-4941

CONSULATES—OFF MAP

Cyprus	2933 Wbstr (O)	893-1661	**India**	540 Arguello	668-0662
Fiji	6620 Tlgrph (O)	654-3970	**Malta**	2564 Sn Bruno	468-4321
Haiti	430 Monterey	469-5629	**Nauru**	2333 Hrson (O)	832-5249
Iceland	3150 20th Ave	564-4007	**Spain**	2080 Jefferson	922-2995

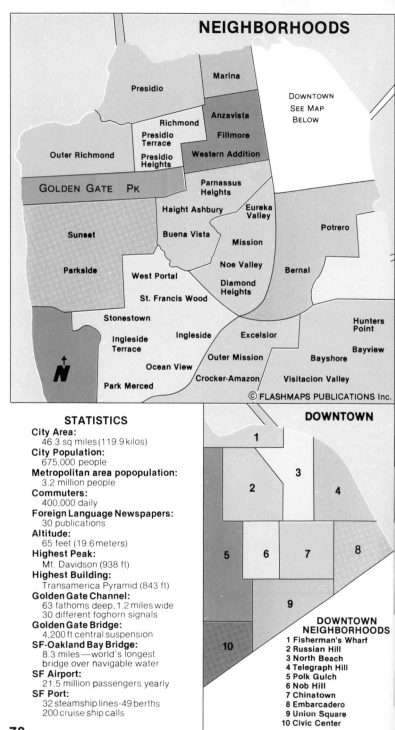

NEIGHBORHOODS

Marina

DOWNTOWN
SEE MAP
BELOW

Presidio

Anzavista

Richmond

Fillmore

Presidio
Terrace

Western Addition

Outer Richmond

Presidio
Heights

GOLDEN GATE PK

Parnassus
Heights

Eureka
Valley

Haight Ashbury

Potrero

Buena Vista

Sunset

Mission

Noe Valley

Parkside

West Portal

Diamond
Heights

Bernal

St. Francis Wood

Stonestown

Hunters
Point

Ingleside
Terrace

Ingleside

Excelsior

Bayview

Bayshore

N

Ocean View

Outer Mission

Park Merced

Crocker-Amazon

Visitacion Valley

© FLASHMAPS PUBLICATIONS Inc.

STATISTICS

City Area:
46.3 sq miles (119.9 kilos)

City Population:
675,000 people

Metropolitan area popopulation:
3.2 million people

Commuters:
400,000 daily

Foreign Language Newspapers:
30 publications

Altitude:
65 feet (19.6 meters)

Highest Peak:
Mt. Davidson (938 ft)

Highest Building:
Transamerica Pyramid (843 ft)

Golden Gate Channel:
63 fathoms deep, 1.2 miles wide
30 different foghorn signals

Golden Gate Bridge:
4,200 ft central suspension

SF-Oakland Bay Bridge:
8.3 miles—world's longest
bridge over navigable water

SF Airport:
21.5 million passengers yearly

SF Port:
32 steamship lines-49 berths
200 cruise ship calls

DOWNTOWN

DOWNTOWN NEIGHBORHOODS

1 Fisherman's Wharf
2 Russian Hill
3 North Beach
4 Telegraph Hill
5 Polk Gulch
6 Nob Hill
7 Chinatown
8 Embarcadero
9 Union Square
10 Civic Center

SAN FRANCISCO AREA COMMUNITIES

Community	Approx Miles Center SF	Bridges and Main Arteries to Area	Public Transportation BART/Buses/So Pacific RR
Alameda	12	Bay Bridge to 17	Bart/E Bay,Transbay
Albany	14	Bay Bridge/80	Bart/East Bay*
Antioch	45	Bay Bridge to 24,242,4	Bart/East Bay*
Belmont	24	280 or 101 to 92	Bart/SamTrans,SPRR*
Benicia	36	Bay Bridge/80 to 780	Bart/Greyhound
Berkeley	12	Bay Bridge/80	Bart/AC Trans*
Brisbane	7	101	Bart/SamTrans,SPRR*
Burlingame	16	101	Bart/SamTrans,SPRR*
Castro Valley	28	Bay Bridge to 580	Bart/AC Trans
Concord	32	Bay Bridge to 24,680	Bart/Greyhound
Corte Madera	16	Golden Gate Bridge/101	Golden Gate Trans
Daly City	8	1, 280	Bart/SamTrans
El Cerrito	15	Bay Bridge/80	Bart/AC Trans*
Emeryville	9	Bay Bridge/80	Bart/AC Trans
Fairfield	45	Bay Bridge/80	Greyhound
Foster City	21.5	101 to 92	SamTrans
Fremont	35	Bay Bridge to 17	Bart/Greyhound
Half Moon Bay	30	208 to 92	SamTrans
Hayward	33	101 to 92 or Bay Brdg to 17	Bart/AC Trans*
Lafayette	20	Bay Bridge to 24	Bart/Greyhound
Los Altos	43	280	SamTrans,SPRR
Martinez	29	Bay Bridge/80,4	Bart/Greyhound
Menlo Park	30	101 to 82	SamTrans,SPRR*
Millbrae	16	280	SamTrans, SPRR
Moraga	19	Bay Brdg,24 to Moraga Way	Bart/AC Trans
Napa	41	Bay Bridge/80 to 29	Greyhound
Newark	37	101 to 84	Bart
Novato	31	Golden Gate Bridge/101	Golden Gate Trans*
Oakland	10	Bay Bridge/80 to 580	Bart/AC Trans
Orinda	15	Bay Bridge to 24	Bart/Greyhound
Pacifica	14	280 to 1	SamTrans
Palo Alto	32	101 or 280 to G3	SamTrans,SPRR*
Petaluma	43	Golden Gate Bridge/101	Golden Gate Trans*
Pittsburg	40	Bay Bridge/80 to 4	Bart/Greyhound
Pleasant Hill	28	Bay Bridge to 24,680	Bart/Greyhound
Pleasanton	47	Bay Bridge to 580,680	Greyhound
Redwood City	29	101/280 to 84	SamTrans,SPRR*
Richmond	16.5	Bay Bridge/80	Bart/AC Trans*
San Anselmo	21	Golden Gate/101,Drake Hwy	Golden Gate Trans
San Bruno	11	101 or 280 to 380	SamTrans, SPRR
San Carlos	26	101	SamTrans,SPRR*
San Jose	50	101, 280	Greyhound,SPRR
San Leandro	23	Bay Bridge to 17	Bart/AC Trans*
San Mateo	20	101	SamTrans,SPRR*
San Rafael	19.5	Golden Gate Brdg/101	Golden Gate Trans*
Santa Clara	48	101/280 to 17	Greyhound,SPRR
Santa Rosa	55	Golden Gate Bridge/101	Golden Gate Trans*
Sausalito	10	Golden Gate Bridge/101	Golden Gate Trans
Sebastopol	51	Golden Gate Bridge/101,116	Golden Gate Trans*
So San Francisco	10	101	SamTrans,SPRR*
Sonoma	44	Golden Gate Brdg/101,37,121	Greyhound
Sunnyvale	45	101/280 to 85	Greyhound,SPRR
Tiburon	18	Golden Gate/101,Tiburon Blvd	Golden Gate Trans
Vallejo	30.5	Bay Bridge/80	Greyhound
Walnut Creek	24	Bay Bridge to 24	Bart/Greyhound

*Also Greyhound Bus Line

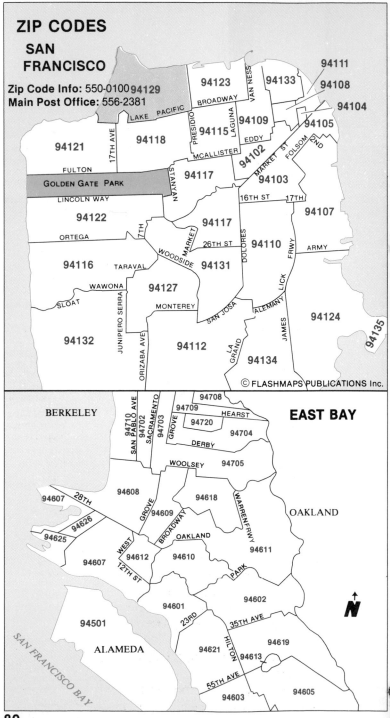

ZIP CODES

SAN FRANCISCO

Zip Code Info: 550-0100
Main Post Office: 556-2381

94129

94123
94133
94111
94108
94104
VAN NESS
BROADWAY
94109
94105
LAGUNA
94115
EDDY
PRESIDIO
LAKE   PACIFIC
17TH AVE
94121
94118
MCALLISTER
94102
MARKET ST
FOLSOM
2ND
FULTON
STANYAN
94117
94103
GOLDEN GATE PARK
16TH ST
17TH
LINCOLN WAY
94107
94122
94117
DOLORES
ORTEGA
7TH
MARKET
26TH ST
94110
ARMY
WOODSIDE
FRWY
94116
TARAVAL
94131
LICK
WAWONA
94127
SLOAT
JUNIPERO SERRA
MONTEREY
SAN JOSA
ALEMANY
JAMES
94124
94132
ORIZABA AVE
94112
LA GRAND
94134
94135

© FLASHMAPS PUBLICATIONS Inc.

EAST BAY

BERKELEY
94708
94709
94710
SAN PABLO AVE
SACRAMENTO
94702
94703
GROVE
94720
HEARST
94704
DERBY
94705
WOOLSEY
94608
GROVE
94618
WARREN FRWY
OAKLAND
94607
28TH
94609
94626
94625
WEST
BROADWAY
94611
94607
94612
OAKLAND
94610
PARK
12TH ST
94601
94602
N
94501
23RD
35TH AVE
ALAMEDA
94621
94619
HILTON
94613
SAN FRANCISCO BAY
55TH AVE
94603
94605